THE DBT SKILLS WORKBOOK FOR

TEENS

ADHD

Essential Coping Strategies to Develop
Distress Tolerance Skills, Effective Emotional
Regulation Habits, and Strong, Resilient
Interpersonal Relationships

M.A. MARTINE

GET THIS EXCLUSIVE

5-minute Audio Guided Meditation

To help safely **MANAGE YOUR TEEN'S** sudden emotional meltdown.

and more mindfulness resources...

JOURNALS & SELF-CARE PLANERS

COLORING BOOKS

SCAN QR CODE TO GET YOUR COPY

TABLE OF CONTENTS

TABLE OF CONTENTS

TABLE OF CONTENTS

INTRODUCTION

Hi Reader,

I'm glad to finally get through to you on this subject. I've helped a lot of young people with this, but I don't think I am done yet because we haven't met. Now that you have my book in front of you, I'm hoping we can have some interesting interactions as we go through each page.

I've been longing to ask a crucial question as I prepared to write to you: "Why?" Yes, why do you need this therapy? Why do you need this book to educate you about this therapy? Will this therapy make you a better human being? Will this therapy alleviate emotional symptoms partially or completely?

Aren't those the questions you've been asking, too? I know, right? And I know it's the reason you picked this book.

The same question that made you select this book, among many others, motivated me to write it. It's to let you know that this book is for *you*. I put my expertise and years of experience into writing this book with you in mind.

Now, to answer our mutual question, let's get this straight first. Do you need dialectical behavior therapy (DBT)?

You need this therapy if:

✓ You're hyperactive; that is, you have lots of energy or move and talk too much. Or you have difficulty paying attention. Or you act without thinking it through. These are symptoms of a disorder in teens and young adults known as attention deficit hyperactivity disorder (ADHD).

✓ You fidget a lot and barely sit still.

✓ You avoid tasks that require a lot of mental effort like schoolwork or homework.

✓ You don't pay close attention to the details and make "careless" mistakes.

✓ You have trouble following instructions and finishing tasks like chores or homework.

✓ Small things like sosound outside the window often distract you.

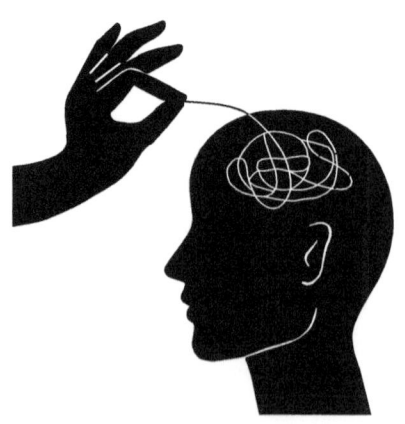

✓ You have trouble remembering everyday hings. You constantly experience extreme mood swings and uncontrollable emotions. Such experiences are related to a disorder known as Borderline personality disorder (BPD).

✓ To cope with emotional pain, you harm your body by cutting your skin.

✓ You have a mental health issue that may have developed after a scary, shocking, dangerous, or life-threatening event. This mental health issue is usually termed Post-traumatic stress disorder (PTSD).

✓ Your eating pattern is abnormal, like eating large amounts of food when you're not hungry or you eat in large quantities to get rid of it later. It could also be that you eat way faster than every other person, or you eat till you feel uncomfortable. That's known as a binge eating pattern.

✓ You're always anxious.

If you fall into any of the categories above, don't drop this book. But if you don't belong to any of those, don't drop it just yet. You're about to become a solution provider for someone who needs this book.

If the list above is any indication, you could benefit from some assistance in overcoming these abnormalities. On a scale of 1 to 10, this therapeutic option I'm about to share with you rates a 9 in its effectiveness in transforming you into a happier kid, a healthy young adult, and a loving human.

Here is a stat to support my claim:

✓ BMC Psychiatry found that after finishing the group treatment, 88% of the participants reported that they could better control symptoms of ADHD.

Note that in my years of working with ADHD patients and other disorders using dialectical behavioral therapy, I discovered that this therapeutic option works best for those committed to the process.

So, I'd like to know before we continue:

✓ Do you like your current state or want to be a better, healthy person?

✓ How many resources can you commit to becoming the better, healthier, and more organized person you've been dreaming of?

So, if you desire,

✓ to learn life-long coping skills

✓ how to calmly interact with people in your life – in a good way

✓ to feel and live happier

- ✓ to be more productive

- ✓ to improve chronic stress

- ✓ to stop negative habits

- ✓ to be healthier

I recommend that you make a firm commitment to practice every piece of information I uncover in the chapters of this book as they apply to you.

WHAT'S MORE?

I've only introduced the theme of this book here, but there's a whole lot more you can learn in this book. You'll get to know more about DBT and its benefits to you. You'll also get to know why this therapeutic option works. You'll learn how it works and how to apply it to your context.

You won't be the last person I take on this transformational journey, but you're one of the most important people I'm glad to have along for the ride. I'm not done in this spatiotemporal realm until I've seen you become the best version of yourself. This book is just a step in that direction.

Finally, I know what it means to have one of those behavioral, mental, or emotional disorders. I've seen and experienced it. Nothing is more implausible than when these disorders persist, they make you believe that's just how you were born and there's nothing you can do about it. However, that's just a partial fact. There's a flip side. There's a flip side to those disorders.

The good news is that I've seen both sides. And I can tell which of the sides looks good. Right now, you've experienced just one side of that fact. You've seen how ugly and frustrating it could be.

Don't quit just yet. My objective in writing this to you is to take you on an adventure that will help you cross from the side you're on to the other side. On arriving at the other side, what you'll discover will amaze you.

Your current situation doesn't accurately reflect who you really are. There is more to you than you initially realized. These disorders cloud your judgment about your identity and essence. As a result, the images you have been seeing are distorted. Yes, before you ask, I am more aware of who you are and what you are made of. This book aims not only to tell you how lovely you are but also to demonstrate how you can change into what you see.

Now, I know we've only just met, but I have a simple favor to ask of you:

Pick up a blank piece of paper. Boldly write on it two things you hope to accomplish after this journey.

Stick the paper in a visible location at all times. Whenever you pick this book up, take a quick look at what you wrote to keep your goals in mind.

Oh wow, that's three favors I've already asked for. Thank you!

I'm ready to come with you on this adventure. The question is, are you ready?

Best wishes,
Teen Advance

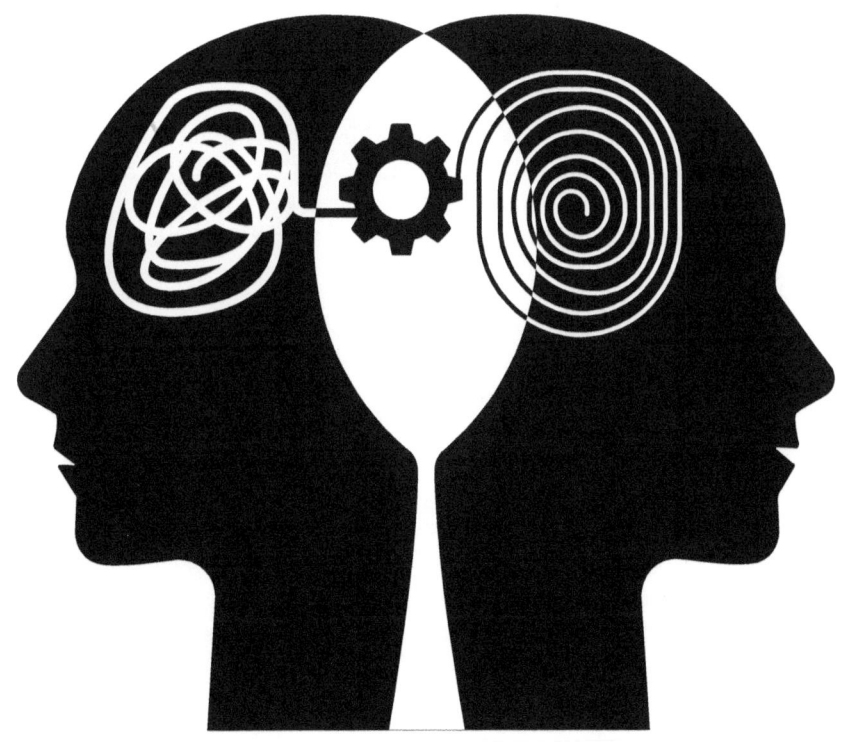

CHAPTER 1: DIALECTICAL BEHAVIOR THERAPY FOR LAYMEN

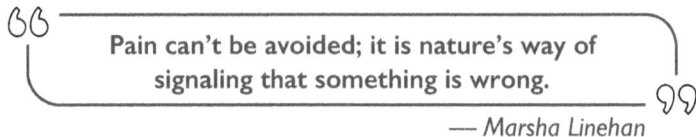

Pain can't be avoided; it is nature's way of signaling that something is wrong.

— *Marsha Linehan*

In an interview, Annie, a female Caucasian, described her 20-year-old life as a "living hell." She was referred from one specialist to another. To alleviate her troubles, she was given psychotropic medications. Instead of helping her get better, the medications only increased her level of depression. Annie began self-medicating to relieve her pain to help herself. But she eventually got addicted to those pain medications.

As a result of the severity of her mental health challenge, Annie was placed on mental health treatment over three years in outpatient and intensive outpatient programs. Although she got a lot of support from her family, they felt helpless at a certain point because Annie continued to struggle with her addiction. Annie's depression level shot up, and as a result, she began to withdraw from her family.

Annie's relationship with her parents was marked by conflict. She became defiant, and it made her parents irritable and concerned. Her condition didn't get any better. She degenerated into constantly yelling at her parents. This was partly because she was in despair. But her parents didn't quit on her. They kept researching an inpatient program that could offer evidence-based treatments. Their search led them to DBT.

Here's the interesting part: after going through four DBT treatment stages, Annie abstained from using pain medication. She had returned to school. Also, she had decided to take a degree in English. She discovered her unique gift for writing poetry, so she decided to take a creative writing class.

Well, therapy could be the last word you want to hear right now. You might even think therapy is only for adults going through a really difficult moment in their lives. Actually, contrary to that, therapies are designed to help every patient—young and old—improve their total well-being. There's no age limit to it. Dialectical behavior therapy (DBT) isn't an exception. With the rising rates of mental stress and behavioral disorders in our society, we could use a lot more therapy.

DBT may be the answer to your behavioral disorder.

Let's bring you up to speed on what DBT is.

INTRODUCTION: UNDERSTANDING DIALECTICAL BEHAVIOR THERAPY

DBT is a type of therapy for people who have trouble controlling their emotions and actions. This could indicate that they experience emotions with greater intensity than other people, which makes them difficult to tolerate. For instance, some teens get angry at the slightest provocation. Usually, they fiercely yell at everyone when angry, and there's nothing anyone can do to appease them. Some kids might go as far as destroying things around them when enraged.

Not everyone with trouble controlling their emotions and actions loves to behave uncontrollably. The kids feel helpless and sometimes sober after their disruptive behavior. To cope with the pain of their emotions, some go as far as cutting their skin, substance abuse, or unhealthy eating.

Those are the kinds of people DBT is designed to help.

When Dr. Marsha Linehan, a suicide researcher, designed this therapy in the late 1970s, she didn't know it would also be effective for helping people with a neurodevelopmental disorder like ADHD until later.

Ever since the evolution of DBT, it has become a well-known method for dealing with emotions and behavior problems. It helps people feel and control their feelings without necessarily acting on them. As an evidence-based treatment, it has been shown through research to be an effective method for treating a wide range of issues.

This treatment isn't just for adults alone; adolescents and pre-teen children with severe emotional difficulties could greatly benefit from this treatment as well.

DBT is an alternative treatment for problems that cognitive-behavioral therapy (CBT) alone can't solve. DBT is tailored to treat the more complex issues of self-harm and emotion dysregulation, drawing heavily on these behavioral treatments.

DBT'S APPROACH

The approach of DBT to treating patients is deeply rooted in the definition of the word "dialectic." It means combining opposing ideas to come up with a positive resolution. In this case, the contrasting ideas are acceptance and change.

On the surface, these two concepts don't seem to mix. But when used together, they can help people improve their lives. Teenage issues like depression, self-harm, and suicidal ideation may be magnified by adolescent therapists' efforts to help them change their thought, emotion, and behavior patterns and their ability to tolerate distress, validate emotions, and accept things as they are. In a comprehensive DBT program, these ideas are incorporated into each component and emphasized throughout treatment.

So, the therapist focuses on helping the patient accept the realities of their current state and then helps them explore ways they'd like to change those negative behaviors. Therefore, in DBT, you accept the reality of your life and behaviors. And as an active participant in the process, you get to learn ways to change your life.

WHAT! HOW COULD I HAVE A DISORDER?

That's the kind of response we get after diagnosing our patients' emotional and/or behavioral disorders. Though they know things are not right with them, accepting the results of the diagnosis to determine what types of treatment they'll get is usually hard for many people.

This is to validate the acceptance of the condition as a valid aspect of treatment. For instance, Catelyn had tried different change-focused therapies, but to no avail. On opting for DBT, she realized DBT skills have a unique feature absent in other therapies she had tried. She referred to it as a "dynamic dance" with acceptance and change. She understood that she wouldn't have gotten much from DBT without the acceptance skills.

According to the *Child Mind Institute*, children, teens, and young adults who struggle with any or all of the following have benefited from DBT:

- ✓ Behaviors that are impulsive or disruptive
- ✓ Frequent mood swings
- ✓ Self-harming and suicidal thoughts and actions
- ✓ Depression and anxiety
- ✓ Conflict with family and friends

- ✓ Outbursts of anger
- ✓ Eating disorders
- ✓ Drug or alcohol abuse
- ✓ Poor coping skills

DOES DBT HAVE A GOAL?

Yes! DBT aims to help people understand the connections between their thoughts, feelings, and actions and how changing negative thought and action patterns can improve their feelings.

WHAT DBT ISN'T

- ✓ **DBT isn't a quick-fix therapy.** It was after about six months into DBT that Dephanee only felt a tinge benefit of the treatment he began six months ago. He felt discouraged and hopeless during those periods of no change. But he held on, and he kept trusting the process.

  I guarantee that DBT has an answer to your question. But don't think that you'll immediately begin to experience transformation once you get started. *Nah.* Patience is a virtue you need to adorn to get the full benefits of DBT.

  Just before you conclude that DBT isn't for you, give it a little more time. And don't forget to check those goals you wrote down on the sheet constantly. It could be of great help.

- ✓ **DBT isn't a cure.** When you think of a cure for something, you think of a medicine that can rid you of certain sickness or disease symptoms. You know you're healed when you no longer feel those symptoms. DBT won't do that for you.

  DBT won't rid you of your emotions. It'll teach you skills that will give you control over your emotions.

For instance, you won't suddenly stop getting angry, but how you react when you get angry after learning DBT skills will be different from how you used to behave before. When you suddenly feel like gulping down large quantities of uncontrollable food, you'll know how to curb that feeling after learning DBT skills.

So, you see, it would be unjust for DBT to take away your emotions. That's what makes you human, isn't it?

✓ **DBT isn't an escape from reality.** In fact, it's an acceptance of reality. Self-harm, substance use, excessive eating, and the like are all ways of escaping reality. But you'll discover that after these escape mediums have taken their full effect and you're now calm, what you tried to escape from hasn't left. It's still present with you. So, what those mediums do is just suppress your reality.

But DBT teaches you first to accept your reality instead of running in futility from it or, worse, suppressing it. Haven't you done more harm to yourself by trying to suppress your reality?

✓ **DBT isn't a one-time fix.** Catelyn accepted that the DBT program was incorporated into her daily life. It's not a one-time change program she could check off her to-do list and move on with her life. She woke up daily to dance with acceptance and change.

Another success story with DBT, Vikkie, said that DBT was a life kit to stay afloat as she continued to evolve into a better version of herself. She said skills like mindfulness and tools like the crisis tool from DBT were things she could take away with her and keep practicing every waking moment.

You're in for a lifelong transformational journey, friend. And just like Alvin Toffler rightly said, learning, unlearning, and relearning are the goals of the 21st century's education program. And those three processes take time.

Regardless of how long it'll take, you're up for it.

I'd advise you not to focus on how long it'll take you to change but rather focus on the process. Your transformation and emergence are in the process.

COMPONENTS OF DBT

A comprehensive DBT program has four result-oriented components. They consist of the following: group skills training, one-on-one therapy, DBT phone coaching, and team consultation.

1. DBT SKILLS TRAINING GROUP

This technique focuses on teaching clients behavioral skills to improve their capabilities. The group is run like a class, with the leader teaching the skills and giving clients homework to do so they can practice using the skills in their daily lives. The full skills curriculum is typically repeated to create a one-year program, and groups meet for approximately 2.5 hours each week. It takes 24 weeks to complete the curriculum, which is repeated.

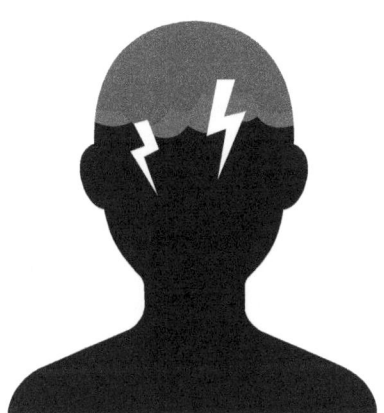

That's just a glimpse of what to expect in a DBT skills training group. Vaughn (2022) took it further. She created a template we can adopt to run a group session. For effectiveness, she suggested that:

✓ A DBT Skills Group should have a leader and a co-leader

✓ Group should last up to 1.5-2.5 hours

✓ Group members who are unable to contain their open hostility toward others are not permitted.

She also suggested these rules to keep the program highly disciplined and efficient.

✓ A member is out of the group if they miss four sessions in a row.

✓ Members of the group must support one another.

✓ Members of the group must contact the leader if they'll be late or absent.

✓ Members of the group mustn't tempt one another.

✓ Members of the group mustn't form confidential or sexual relationships with one another.

✓ Members of the group have an individual therapist if they are suicidal or have severe disorders.

✓ Members of the group act sober.

2. INDIVIDUAL DBT THERAPY

This focuses on motivating clients and assisting them in applying the skills to specific life challenges and events. Individual therapy takes place once a week for approximately 60 minutes under the standard DBT model, concurrent with skills groups.

This will foster a strong connection between the guide/specialist and client through week-after-week meetings. Individual treatment assists a client with remaining on track and inspired all through treatment. Additionally, individual treatment gives down-to-earth solutions to specific issues.

3. PHONE COACHING

DBT phone coaching aims to give clients coaching on how to use skills to deal with difficult situations in their daily lives effectively. Between sessions, clients can call their individual therapist to get coaching when they need it most.

4. DBT THERAPIST CONSULTATION TEAM

This is meant to be therapy for the therapists and to help DBT providers work with people who frequently have severe, complicated, and hard-to-treat disorders. The purpose of the consultation team is to assist therapists in maintaining their competence and motivation to provide the best possible treatment. Teams consist of individual therapists and group leaders who share responsibility for each client's care and typically meet weekly.

Coordinating these DBT components gives the specialist a superior method for interacting with a client regularly and during emergencies.

BENEFITS OF DIALECTICAL BEHAVIOR THERAPY

1. YOU'LL FIND YOURSELF

The primary focus of this therapy is you. Every activity, task, assignment, tool, and medium is designed to work for your good. Throughout the process, the specialist who guides you through it will focus on an image of you. It's the picture of you as a beautiful, loving, emotionally stable, and healthy human being that he keeps in mind.

Therefore, every session he has with you is to help you find yourself. DBT hasn't done its job completely until you discover your real essence.

2. YOUR RELATIONSHIPS WILL IMPROVE

Having a strong support system is essential when dealing with mental health issues. This is overlooked by many types of therapy, which assume that you'll handle things on your own. However, DBT emphasizes the significance of your social relationships in overcoming obstacles.

Building healthy relationships with trust, respectful boundaries, and respect for one another greatly impacts your health and well-being.

You'll notice that you can better manage your relationships as you participate in DBT therapy. This means that you can begin to heal your relationships. You can recover from your addiction, learn how to be more effective in personal interactions, and realize that the people in your life want to help you recover.

3. THE QUALITY OF YOUR LIFE INCREASES

One of DBT's primary goals is to enhance your quality of life. We can't always control what happens to us, but we can control how we respond to it. Our response to it is what determines the quality of our lives.

One of the things you'll enjoy in DBT is the acceptance of the fact that mental health issues are a part of life for some people. Knowing this is essential to moving forward. But that's not all. DBT gently assists patients in making changes that will move them in the right direction and let them know that it's okay to find things challenging.

DBT will help you cope with difficult or negative situations. In addition to putting you on the road to recovery, DBT teaches you how to be your best self no matter what happens.

4. YOUR UNDERSTANDING OF YOUR FEELINGS AND THOUGHTS INCREASES

DBT is a form of cognitive behavioral therapy that focuses on "dialectics," or the use of dialogue to work through current symptoms and past traumas. You become aware of the complex emotions and thought structures that influence your behavior and choices as a result of DBT treatment.

You can make healthy choices when fully comprehending your feelings and mental assumptions. DBT enhances mindfulness, allowing you to remain rooted in the present and focus fully and calmly on your surroundings as well as the situation at hand. Learn ways to keep your thoughts and actions positive. DBT improves your interpersonal effectiveness, communication skills, and ability to handle conflict and distress.

You'll build a comprehensive set of methods you can use in everyday life and difficult situations.

5. YOU'LL BE ABLE TO DEAL WITH POTENTIAL TRIGGERS IN A HEALTHY WAY

You will learn how to deal with painful emotional triggers. When you learn the principles of DBT, you can control the inner triggers that threaten your serenity. You can let go of anger, fear, anxiety, loss, stress, and even trauma.

6. THE SKILLS GO BEYOND MENTAL ILLNESS

DBT's goal is to alleviate the symptoms of mental illness, but it doesn't stop there. The DBT therapist teaches skills useful in many other areas of life. For instance, numerous other facets of health and well-being are linked by research to mindfulness. This ability can be beneficial in various settings, including at work, at home, and while having fun.

You can enhance other areas of your life. Even though you're taking DBT to help you recover, you'll find it applicable to many different aspects of your mental health and that what you learn will benefit your wholeness. Your mental health is central to your functionality.

ADDITIONAL BENEFITS OF DBT INCLUDE THE FOLLOWING:

- ✓ It'll guide you to change unhealthy patterns of behavior into healthy ones

- ✓ It'll help you recognize your strengths and put them to use in all aspects of your life.

- ✓ It'll teach you to improve your communication skills

- ✓ It'll assist you in gaining a stronger sense of control over your relationships, life, and emotions.

- ✓ It'll show you how to change your negative thought processes, so you don't act impulsively.

- ✓ It'll teach you to prioritize—say no and ask for what you want.

- ✓ It'll improve emotional regulation and self-care through the application of mindfulness techniques. You'll get better at paying attention to what's happening inside and around you. You'll be able to make rational decisions instead of impulsive ones with the assistance of this therapy.

- ✓ Understanding your distress tolerance can assist you in determining what you can and cannot change. Instead of making decisions based on how you feel or think about a situation, you make decisions based on facts and logic.

THE PROS AND CONS OF DIALECTICAL BEHAVIORAL THERAPY

While DBT can be highly effective for some individuals, it may be ineffective for others. Thus, DBT also has its advantages and disadvantages. What's advantageous to you might not be to another.

Here are some of the advantages of DBT you need to know:

- ✓ It is thorough: DBT is an intensive type of therapy focusing on getting results quickly from the first day.

- ✓ Reduces hospitalizations, self-injury, and the seriousness of borderline personality disorder (BPD) symptoms significantly.

- ✓ Boosts self-esteem and respect.

- ✓ Improves emotion control.

- ✓ Reduces avoidance through experience.

- ✓ Reduces assertive rage.

- ✓ Tools for Managing Stress: The patient in DBT is taught techniques for managing stress, such as mindfulness. This is especially helpful because it teaches the patient to remain calm and grounded in the present moment during challenging times.

- ✓ Low rate of dropouts: In contrast to many other types of therapy, DBT appears to have a low dropout rate, indicating that the majority of patients will complete treatment. This suggests that DBT works very well.

- ✓ Therapy and medication together: Medication is often used to treat borderline personality disorder. Therapy and medication can be used together to great effect.

- ✓ Zen Buddhist mindfulness techniques are incorporated into DBT, which may pique the interest of spiritual seekers.

- ✓ Through the phone coaching component, participants have access to their clinician round-the-clock in the event of a crisis or for immediate guidance during difficult times as an additional layer of support.

- ✓ Participants in the weekly DBT skills training group therapy sessions have access to an emotionally secure setting in which they can begin to apply the DBT skills alongside others working on issues similar to their own.

- ✓ DBT, an evidence-based treatment, improves people's quality of life and goes beyond mental illness.

THE DISADVANTAGES OF DBT INCLUDE:

✓ It's not a quick fix: Changing deeply ingrained emotions and thoughts takes time. Even though change can occur almost immediately, DBT won't give you all the benefits right away.

✓ It requires commitment: DBT necessitates a strong commitment to therapy. A person is expected to commit to the entire duration of the therapy, which can last up to 30 sessions. The number of sessions may vary, though.

✓ Because mindfulness practice based on Zen Buddhist teachings forms the basis of DBT, some clients (such as conservative Jews, Christians, Muslims, and so on) may be opposed to DBT's elements based on Eastern religious philosophies.

✓ Assignments corresponding to the DBT skills taught or visited during each session are essential to the weekly DBT skills training group therapy sessions, which some may find burdensome.

✓ Problems with group settings: As previously stated, receiving DBT in a group setting may be beneficial but may not be appropriate for all individuals. Additionally, it means that the patient does not receive the individual attention that one-on-one sessions do.

✓ It can bring back memories: DBT focuses on the present in some areas but also on past events in others. This could be traumatizing, but a therapist will ensure you feel at ease.

✓ The numerous DBT skills may appear overwhelming and discouraging. As a result, some people who would benefit greatly from dialectical behavior therapy consider it too complicated and are reluctant to try it.

These are the basic things I consider important for you to know about DBT.

Have you started taking notes yet? Here's a quick recap of what you've read in this chapter: I introduced you to the creator of DBT, Dr. Marsha Linehan, and the reason DBT was created. You've got to know that DBT isn't for everyone; it's just for a specific group who need extra help controlling their emotions and injurious behavior patterns. DBT isn't a person; it's just a handy tool set you can take along anywhere you go. Don't fret; DBT isn't a burden you need to include in your daily routine; in fact, it'll help you ease the stress you've been bearing. And this comes with some other amazing benefits, too.

Remember that I told you not to think of DBT as a fix-it-all tool because it's not.

Now, let's take a quick look at what you've got:

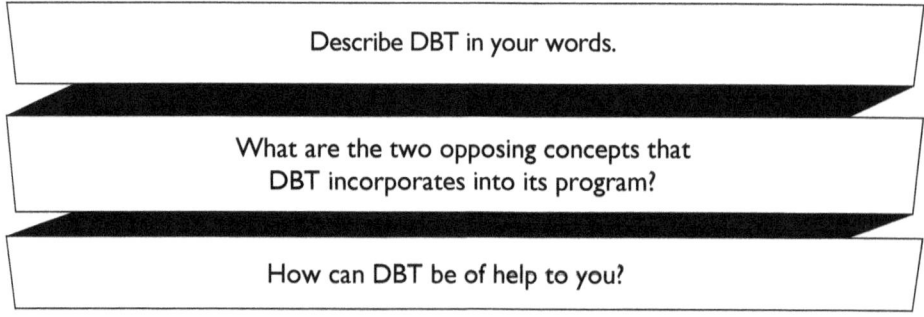

Describe DBT in your words.

What are the two opposing concepts that DBT incorporates into its program?

How can DBT be of help to you?

CHAPTER 2: WHY DIALECTICAL BEHAVIOR THERAPY WORKS

> 66 Live the actual moment. Only this actual moment is life. 99
> — *Thích Nhất Hạnh*

In my semi-short note, I listed categories of people who need DBT. You'll notice that I didn't write an extensive explanation for any of those mental or behavioral patterns. I just highlighted them. In this chapter, I'll narrow it down to a particular behavioral pattern evident in several children and teenagers. Young adults are not excluded anyway.

Rosa, from Wellington, New Zealand, shared her struggles as a young girl diagnosed with attention deficit hyperactivity disorder (ADHD). Before she was diagnosed with this disorder, she was perceived as a loud, unbearable, and genuinely indifferent child. Her sports coaches had issues with her. They frequently complained about how difficult it was to coach her. The same was true for her instructors.

She experienced similar difficulties at home, too. Every time she tried to discuss essays and tests with her dad, he would get angry when she lost focus or started staring at other things. She frequently misplaced her laptop, her school lunch box, and sports practice equipment. She was constantly blamed for losing things and getting them back.

Rosa exhibited symptoms of a disorder known as attention deficit hyperactivity disorder (ADHD). We'll just stick to the acronym hereafter.

Let's drive this home. Before we go into how DBT can be used to correct ADHD, let's talk about some of the *ADHD symptoms* that ADHD Ireland highlighted:

✓ **Self-centered behavior.** An inability to recognize the wants and needs of other people is a common symptom of ADHD. This could be displayed when you're having trouble waiting for your turn and/or you impatiently interrupt a procedure, a conversation, or a game you weren't part of. You're focused on your interest alone.

✓ **Mood swings.** Teens with ADHD might have trouble controlling their emotions. They might become annoyed at inappropriate times. Younger children may throw tantrums.

✓ **Fidgeting.** ADHD teens frequently have trouble staying still. When forced to sit, they might try to get up and run around, fidget, or squirm in their chair. When they fidget, playing quietly or relaxing during leisure activities becomes difficult.

✓ **Unfinished tasks.** Teens with ADHD may be interested in various things but have difficulty finishing them. For instance, they can begin assignments, chores, or projects but move on to the next thing that interests them before completing them. Even when someone is speaking directly to them, a teenager with ADHD may have trouble paying attention. They will claim to have heard you, but they won't be able to repeat what you said.

✓ **Avoidance of tasks requiring a sustained mental effort.** This same lack of focus can lead to a teenager avoiding tasks like paying attention in class or doing homework that requires a sustained mental effort.

✓ **Difficulty adhering to instructions.** Teens with ADHD may have difficulty adhering to instructions that necessitate planning or carrying out a plan. This may result in careless errors but does not indicate laziness or intelligence deficit.

✓ **Escape from reality.** Teens with ADHD who daydream (introverts are found doing this mostly) are not always boisterous and loud. Being quieter and less involved than other kids is another sign of ADHD. A teenager with ADHD may avoid paying attention to the world around them. They daydream or stare into space.

✓ **Disorganized.** An ADHD teen may have trouble keeping track of activities and tasks. They may have difficulty setting priorities for homework, school projects, and other assignments. This could land them in trouble at school.

✓ **Forgetting Things.** Teenagers with ADHD may forget things in their daily lives. They might neglect their chores or homework. They might also frequently misplace things.

NOTE: A teenager with ADHD will exhibit symptoms in multiple contexts. For instance, they might appear distracted at home and in school.

Every child, teenager, or young adult has exhibited one or two of these symptoms at some point. However, it becomes something to act on if those symptoms become regular or affect school performance and/or relationships with others.

DBT FOR ATTENTION DEFICIT HYPERACTIVITY DISORDER

The DBT Center of Marin stated that 9.4% of children aged 17 and younger had been diagnosed with ADHD. Fascinating, right? The good thing about this is that ADHD can be treated.

Many conditions with such features as an inability to control emotions, such as ADHD, mood and anxiety disorders, etc., can be successfully treated with DBT.

Wasn't DBT designed to treat borderline personality disorder? Yes, so it seemed. Before it was adapted to treat ADHD, DBT was used to treat various mental illnesses.

Do you remember Marsha Linehan? The brain behind DBT? Yes, that's right. When she created DBT, it was designed for individuals diagnosed with Borderline personality disorder (BPD). DBT was created to help people recover from emotional outbursts, such as self-harming behaviors.

But do you also remember that the main feature of BPD is emotional dysregulation? DBT has been demonstrated to be a successful treatment for all the illnesses since they are all characterized by an inability to manage emotions, including attention deficit disorder (ADHD or ADD), mood and anxiety disorders, and substance use disorders. It is now a standard treatment for ADHD.

HOW DOES DBT HELP WITH ADHD?

A dialectical approach to things leads to a balanced view of things. When your thoughts, feelings, and life situations are not all running agog, DBT employs a dialectical approach to help you have a more balanced perspective.

I told you about those two odd approaches DBT employs—acceptance and change. Accepting uncomfortable feelings and situations before attempting to change them is a central belief of DBT. This approach is effective in helping ADHD patients agree with their therapists to develop a recovery strategy by accepting the existence of troubling thoughts and feelings.

For instance, an ADHD patient who struggles to concentrate while studying can be taught to adapt her thinking style and change her study routine. So let's say she wants to study for one hour. She can't concentrate for that period. She has to accept that reality first. But instead of forcing her to try harder, a dialectical approach will encourage her to change her studying routine. So, instead of studying for one hour non-stop, she would study for 30 minutes. She'll take a 10-minute break and then continue studying for another 30 minutes.

She'll discover that she'll accomplish significantly more in two shorter periods than in one full stretch.

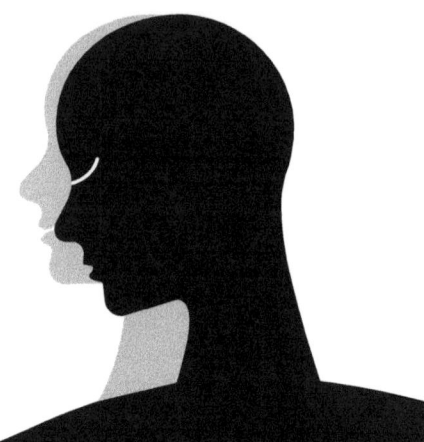

DIALECTICAL BEHAVIOR THERAPY FOR TEENS AND YOUNG ADULTS

According to Brillante (2020), DBT's main objective is to assist young people in creating a worthwhile life. Teenagers who experience depression, severe family conflict, or trouble controlling their emotions may occasionally believe that their life is not worth living, especially if these issues have persisted for a long time.

There are primary areas of challenge that adolescent DBT seeks to address. Addressing them could help young people decide in what direction they want their lives to go.

Can you relate to any of the issues below? The list below summarizes the major issues resulting from disordered mental and behavioral patterns in teens and young adults. These and many more are why we have distraught young people in our communities today.

A CONFUSED SELF

You could get stuck in the past when you're unsure about your emotions and don't understand your thoughts. This could also rack up a lot of fear about what the future holds for you.

With those thought patterns, it'll be difficult for you to ever appreciate your present moment, not to talk of focusing on it.

This could also make teens lose a sense of their individual values and goals.

CONFUSED SELF IMAGE

It's difficult to identify who you really are if you have unstable emotions you don't have any control over. Before people identify you by your emotional reaction, you will have convinced yourself that your emotional and mental behavioral patterns are just who you are.

The question is, can you see the beauty of a stream when it's troubled? If you answered no, it implies that your beauty and true identity aren't in your troubled state. Your negative behavioral pattern gives you a false view of your image.

ABNORMAL EMOTIONAL DISPLAY

This is otherwise known as emotional dysregulation. This happens when a person experiences intense emotions but has limited control over how they are managed and how they behave as a result. This could be a sudden, intense change in mood or a negative emotional state that lasts for a long time, like depression.

THOUGHTLESS ACTIONS

I've worked with young adults who are highly impulsive. I feel compassion for them whenever I realize their helplessness. Looking past their emotional outburst will show how vulnerable they are inside. As a matter of fact, some of those actions are borne out of frustration.

Acting impulsively means acting on an urge or emotion without thinking about what might happen or what might happen next. Substance use, self-harm, impulsive eating, and verbal or physical outbursts fueled by anger are examples of impulsive actions. These actions may be taken to avoid or escape difficult emotional situations.

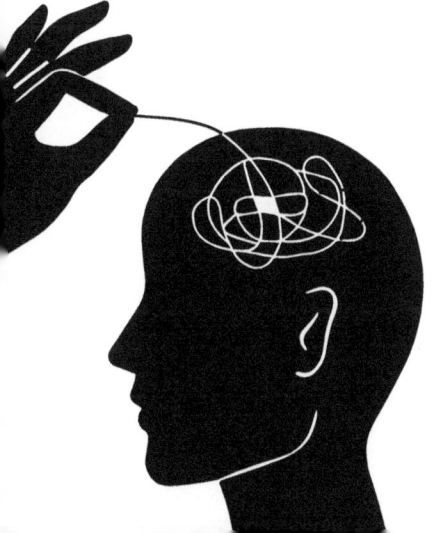

TOXIC RELATIONSHIPS

You can't expect an impulsive teenager to have a healthy relationship, can you? There will always be one issue after another with one's peers. Due to how relationships have been negatively impacted, interpersonal challenges may result in difficulty maintaining healthy relationships, a lot of conflict in relationships, and potential loneliness.

This could result in difficulty maintaining self-respect under peer pressure, expressing one's needs, and saying no to others.

PROBLEMS FOR FAMILIES AND TEENS

Virtually every normal child has disagreements with their parents at some point when they are growing up. Teens' disagreements with parents or other family members are common. However, when it becomes a serious disagreement, it's something to be concerned about.

This could result from trouble comprehending each other's feelings, behaviors, or points of view. And just like in other relationships, it could cause relationships with people who should be the first circle of support to go so wrong.

HOW CAN DBT WORK FOR TEENS AND YOUNG ADULTS?

Science is always advancing. And it might interest you to know that researchers see teens' needs, including yours, as distinct from adults.' Therefore, treatments for both age groups should differ.

Here's the good news: Pieper (2020) announced a program validated by research to address the key differences between DBT for adults and DBT for adolescents, DBT-A (DBT for Adolescents). Including caregivers is the most significant distinction between DBT for adolescents and DBT for adults. Caregivers are frequently a part of skills training sessions or may participate in their own sessions.

So, when you're having individual or one-on-one therapy, it'll occasionally include caregivers, as will additional family sessions. Also, you won't be the only one to go through the phone coaching; your caregiver will as well.

Your adolescent stage development is also something to consider in your program. Naturally, most teens have a shorter attention span compared to adults. Therefore, your group sessions will be shortened compared to adults.'

Another consideration is that since people in your age group learn quicker with learning aids like pictures, examples, and metaphors, DBT for teens has been designed to include those elements in your individual and group therapy.

Additionally, skilled therapists will know the distinction between adolescent and adult developmental tasks. This knowledge will be incorporated into the issues being treated for utmost effectiveness.

Some of the methods, which you could also call "skills," employed in DBT to treat teens and young adults include:

✓ **Mindfulness**

This skill teaches you to understand the peculiar symptoms of uncontrolled emotions. It also encourages you to be present and rooted in the moment, not some warped past or a future you don't have access to yet.

You'll learn more about mindfulness in a later chapter.

✓ **Self-acceptance**

Acceptance, as I've stated before, is paramount to your transformation. Self-acceptance is an offshoot of mindfulness. It teaches you to fully accept what is happening or has happened. This does not mean you're okay with what has been happening to you; it just means that you're no longer living in self-denial of your reality. You accept that it's a disorder. And it's simply a disorder that can be reorganized. This method can free you from fighting reality.

Before you go further, can you take a moment to reflect on those injurious behavioral patterns? Don't deny their existence because they do exist, and you've been exhibiting them.

Confront yourself with the truth, like "It's true I get angry excessively." "And I yell when I'm really angry."

EMOTION REGULATION SKILLS

Emanuele (cited by Garey, 2022) said that emotion regulation places a significant emphasis on the physical body. Eating right, getting enough sleep, taking medication, and not using drugs are all important. They all have a way of boosting your emotional well-being.

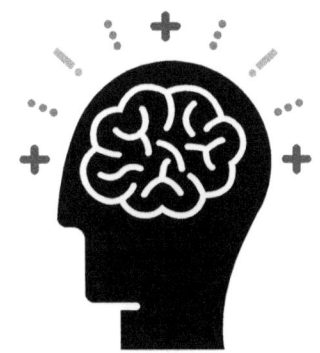

This skill helps you comprehend how emotions work, the urge to act attached to each emotion, and whether to act on these urges.

Note that every feeling you experience serves a particular purpose. You can learn more about your current situation from these emotions.

Don't judge yourself quickly when you notice that you're feeling something. Just observe it. Each emotion has value, even if some are more pleasant than others. Consider what this feeling might be trying to tell you about your situation and identify the emotion you're experiencing. After that, you can respond to the emotion or let it go.

✓ **Opposite Action**

This skill falls under the category of emotion regulation. Teens who struggle with trauma, depression, anxiety, low self-esteem, anger management issues, and other issues can benefit from this skill.

Use the opposite action when you're going through a painful emotion that doesn't fit your particular circumstance or isn't working for you at the moment. Let's say, for instance, that a teen experiences an increased sense of shame each time she enters the class. There was no reason for her to be ashamed because she had done nothing wrong to her teachers or peers. However, her current reality is that each time she enters that class, she experiences feelings of shame, worthlessness, and low self-esteem. As a result, she rarely speaks up or raises her hand in class.

At this time, the opposite action should be taken.

✓ **Walking the Middle Path**

Miller (cited by Garey, 2022) stated that this has to do with acknowledging multiple truths in the worldview of the teenagers and their parents rather than saying, "I'm right, and you're wrong." Through this skill, you and your parents will learn to validate one another, negotiate and compromise, and see things from the other person's perspective.

This skill employs other skills such as dialectics, validation, and behavioral change

DIALECTICS

This method focuses on finding common ground between opposing viewpoints, meaning you value and acknowledge the other person's view instead of castigating them. For instance, someone may be doing their best but still need improvement. Acknowledging their best effort before telling them how they need to improve will inject positive energy into them.

VALIDATION

Recognizing the significance of both your own experience and that of another person is validation. Validation acknowledges one's actions, feelings, and thoughts, regardless of disagreement.

CHANGE IN BEHAVIOR

This is a collection of strategies for motivating, implementing, and sustaining desired behavior changes.

WHAT AGE IS DBT APPROPRIATE FOR?

The DBT program has evolved from treating only adults with mental and behavioral disorders. It can now be used to treat other age groups.

Pieper stated that DBT now has an adapted program for adolescents, DBT-A (DBT for Adolescents). *The Child Mind Institute* has also announced that it has a DBT-adapted program for children and preadolescents. They call it DBT-C. DBT-C is a practical version of DBT for children and preadolescents between 6 and 12. It's an extensive DBT program tailored to meet the requirements of children in this age range.

THE FOUR PILLARS OF DBT

I've touched on these previously. I'll elaborate a little more here. The four pillars of DBT are what Dr. Marsha Linehan, the creator of DBT, also referred to as the "modules" of DBT.

They are:

1. Mindfulness
2. Distress tolerance
3. Interpersonal effectiveness
4. Emotional regulation

Let's have a brief discussion on each of these pillars:

MINDFULNESS

You'll learn more about this pillar in the next chapter. However, let's have a look at what mindfulness is. It's a tool and a skill. This implies that you can learn it.

Mindfulness is a powerful tool designed to make you worry less about the past and future and help you live in the moment.

So, basically, mindfulness will help you to:

✓ Learn to control one's emotions and thoughts.

✓ Acquire the ability to be more aware and to live in the now.

✓ Gain a sense of identity.

DISTRESS TOLERANCE

Even though some of us experience emotional highs and lows that are more frequent and intense, we all have times when they feel big and overwhelming. Distress tolerance skills aim to teach how to get through difficult times without making things worse by providing alternative and proactive responses to situations.

This module helps you accept certain circumstances, thoughts, and feelings that cannot be changed.

Summarily, the distress tolerance module does the following:

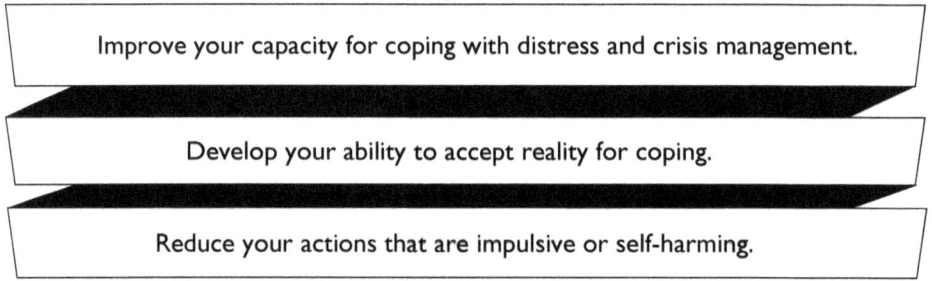

Improve your capacity for coping with distress and crisis management.

Develop your ability to accept reality for coping.

Reduce your actions that are impulsive or self-harming.

INTERPERSONAL EFFECTIVENESS

Every human on the planet has an innate desire for social interaction. But what happens when, in your own way, you've tried several times to establish a connection with someone, yet you continue to feel rejected, hurt, and disappointed?

Naturally, you might observe that you begin to get into more arguments, avoid this individual, or just feel like giving up.

The interpersonal effectiveness module aims to teach how to interact effectively with others, formulate requests that increase your chances of satisfying your needs, and consider your self-respect.

EMOTIONAL REGULATION

The fourth module, emotional regulation, teaches you how to control your emotions rather than let them control you. In this module, you'll learn acceptance of your emotions through reality-checking, opposite actions and behaviors associated with particular emotions, etc.

In summary, you'll

 Figure out ways to feel more secure.

 Gain the ability to feel more cheerful.

32

FOUR STAGES AND TARGETS OF DBT

STAGE ONE

Most clients' reactions in Stage One are frequently negative. They start with seemingly out-of-control behaviors like suicide attempts, self-harm, excessive alcohol and drug use, and other kinds of self-destructive behavior.

Now, moving the client from being out of control to being in control is the primary objective of this stage.

At this stage, you'll work with your therapist or specialist to begin to gain behavioral control and view treatment as a means of improving your mental, physical, and spiritual well-being.

STAGE TWO

At this stage, most clients may experience a sense of quiet desperation. They report still having the impression that they have failed in life, despite the fact that a behavioral approach has controlled their life-threatening behavior. Stage two aims to assist you in transitioning from quiet desperation to a full emotional experience.

Stage two also entails reducing any symptoms related to trauma, such as formal PTSD diagnoses and other traumatic emotional experiences. At this stage, the client's traumatic past is being investigated. This invariably leads to heightened emotion.

Here, you'll need to start finding the inner strength you lost. You will learn to recognize, comprehend, and appropriately manage your emotions.

However, an expert in this program will try to avoid intensifying your emotional experiences from the beginning. That will not make things more difficult for you.

STAGE THREE

The objective of this stage is to learn to live life, trust oneself, develop self-respect and self-worth, develop interpersonal skills, set and reach life goals and find contentment and happiness.

This stage builds on the previous stage.

This is the stage where you'll get to learn how to cope without substances and other harmful behaviors. You'll be encouraged to focus on living the life you were created for. Your creative passions, strength, dreams, and desire for meaningful living all come to the fore at this stage. You'll learn to trust, validate, and be empathic here.

The skill of mindfulness is one of the skills you'll learn at this stage.

STAGE FOUR

Dr. Marsha Linehan designed this stage for those seeking deeper meaning through spiritual existence.

This stage aims to help clients overcome a sense of incompleteness and establish a life with an ongoing capacity for unconditional love, joy, and freedom.

DBT was designed to be complete in helping patients recover completely. If you can be committed to the six-month program of DBT, you'll cross to the other side, where everything is beautiful.

Let's review your objectives for this adventure again to see if you're still on track. *Go check now. ...*

While you're on that, here are a few things you should remember about this chapter:

| DBT is effective for treating ADHD. | ADHD has several symptoms that are not peculiar to children or teens alone. | DBT has practicable tools like mindfulness, distress tolerance, and emotional regulation that can help you surmount the challenges of managing your emotions. | DBT offers every ADHD patient an opportunity to alter the course of their life and choose to be better individuals. |

CAN YOU ATTEMPT THESE QUESTIONS?

1
What is ADHD?

2
Did this chapter mention any symptoms you exhibit as an ADHD patient? If yes, what is it?

3
What are the DBT skills discussed in this chapter?

CHAPTER 3: PUTTING MINDFULNESS SKILL TO USE

> 66
> Emotions are not good, bad, right, or wrong.
> The first step to changing our relationship
> to feelings is to be curious about them and
> the messages they send to us.
> 99

—Lane Pederson

You're not new to *mindfulness,* are you? I know you're not if you haven't skipped any part of this book.

Here's a quick story of Katie and her application of this skill. Katie was surprised to find out that mindfulness, a practice her boyfriend, Tal, had encouraged her to learn, was at the heart of DBT when she first heard about it at the beginning of 2019.

Katie experienced such unbearable anxiety that she just wanted a quick fix or a 60-minute meeting with a therapist who would tell her what to do and she would be fine. She suffered from severe anxiety so much that mindfulness sounded nonsense then.

When she sought the assistance of a therapist specializing in Borderline personality disorder (BPD), her self-diagnosis of anxiety matched the symptoms of BPD.

Guess what her therapist recommended …

WHAT IS MINDFULNESS?

Partington (2021) said that the practice of paying attention where and when you want to pay attention is known as "mindfulness." And she said that mindfulness is a practice like swimming or any other sport. By deliberately and repeatedly focusing on the present moment, you strengthen your mindfulness muscles.

The Hope Therapy and Wellness team (2019) also agreed that being present in the present moment is mindfulness. And being mindful means paying attention to everything that is going on around you: where you are, how you feel, what you see, and what you hear right now.

It's easy to know you're mindful with this simple exercise:

Look around you and feel exactly what is happening right now. What did you see?

If you were overthinking, judging, or worrying about what would happen next, you're not being mindful. Because mindfulness is accepting the present in its entirety without judging, worrying, or feeling anxious about it. You are mindful if you can confirm your current experience.

Doesn't that sound simple?

Well, maybe. Our society shows how much time people spend being mindful and fully present in the now. A lot of people are suffering from stress and anxiety. Here are some statistics to show that:

A stress statistic carried out by the *Single Care* team:

✓ Over three-quarters of adults report experiencing signs of stress, such as headaches, tiredness, or trouble sleeping.

✓ Eighty percent of American workers report experiencing stress at work.

✓ Nearly half of all adults in the United States (49%) claim that stress has had a negative impact on their behavior.

✓ Nearly one in five adults in the United States report declining mental health over the past year.

✓ In a 2020 survey, adults in the United States reported that increased stress had:

Affected their behavior in a negative way (49%)

Caused them to feel more tension in their bodies (21%)

Caused them to "snap" out of anger (20%)

Caused them to have unexpected mood swings (20%).

The American Institute of Stress also reported this:

 77% of people experience stress that has an impact on their physical health

73% of people experience stress that has an impact on their mental health

48% of people have trouble sleeping as a result of stress

33% of people report feeling extremely stressed.

Sadly, the levels of stress experienced by approximately half of all Americans are increasing rather than decreasing.

A lot of people "tune out" from what is actually going on, becoming instead distracted by how they see it, what it means, or what it might mean for them in the future. People are unable to truly live in the present, and as a result, they become perplexed and irritated as to why nothing seems to be under their control.

The skill of mindfulness might sound like an easy option; however, it's a practice that can be applied to any activity you're engaged in. Keep your attention on the task at hand, and if it wanders, stop it and bring it back. That capacity for mindfulness can be developed through practice.

Being completely present in the moment without judging is the essence of mindfulness.

 ## SO WHAT HAS MINDFULNESS GOT TO DO WITH DBT?

Since DBT is about regulating and reordering emotional patterns, mindfulness can help to achieve that easily. This makes mindfulness an essential component of DBT because it helps overcome emotional dysregulation.

Whenever we're not mindful of the present moment, we tend to become overwhelmed by things that other people may find insignificant—even though it may seem like the sky is falling on us. It is essential to acknowledge that when we are not mindful, it is typically not due to the actual event but rather to our interpretation of it.

 # Here's a clear example:

Diana recently started working for a new company. On her first day at work, she accidentally deleted a file she believed her boss would find useful. Diana became overwhelmed with fear right away.

Different thoughts began to run through her mind. Thoughts like:

> "Oh! I'm going to be fired."

> "I will be viewed as stupid and useless by everyone."
> "This is such a shame."

> "There is still $200 in my bank account."

> "I won't be able to find a new job right away because I will be fired today."
> "This is a small town, and everyone hears everything." "I may not find another job, and no one will hire me after this."

> "This is awful." "I won't be able to pay the rent."

> "I don't like anyone in the family because of this." "This is why I'm still single."

"I'm worthless."

Can you relate to Diana's case? Maybe yours was that your mother's tumbler mistakenly fell off your hand. And while you were there, lots of negative thoughts began to run through your mind. You became sweaty and panicky in a jiffy.

Well, you're not alone. You've got a company spread across the globe.

I'm not sure about this, but it sounds like that's how humans naturally respond to things like that. Does that mean we all need a DBT session? Maybe not. DBT becomes required when this behavioral pattern becomes intense and regular.

Just imagine how Diana conjured an entire scenario in her mind from a single incident. She spiraled into panic by assuming she knew what other people thought of her and what the future held.

YOU MIGHT BE WONDERING …
SO, HOW DOES MINDFULNESS
WORK?

The first place to start is, "How does your mind work?"

Badcock et al. (2019) believed that the brain (or the mind) is where human thoughts, feelings, and actions originate. There, a complex network of cells receives information from both the inside and outside of the body and transforms it into how we experience ourselves, the world around us, and our relationships with it.

It's obvious from that scientific discovery, although it's still ongoing, that our minds and activities there affect our entire being.

If our thoughts and feelings affect our behavior and how we relate to ourselves and the world around us, isn't it worthwhile to pay close attention to what goes on in our minds?

This is the essence of mindfulness. This skill will teach you to be aware of your thoughts and feelings. This also implies paying attention to your actions, reactions, and surroundings.

Practicing mindfulness puts you in charge of your feelings. You'll be free from being dragged around by your feelings and tortured by thoughts when you practice mindfulness.

It's a fact that there will always be thoughts in your mind. You can't control that. OK, it looks like you don't believe that. Is it because you read an article about how to control your thoughts?

Well, if anyone had succeeded in trying, no one would be having those "Aha!" moments—an excited reaction to a spontaneous, genius idea that flowed in when you weren't thinking about it.

No one has succeeded in controlling their thoughts. What you can do is direct your awareness in the direction you desire. That's the essence of mindfulness.

You can decide where you want your mind to be and how you want to act by being aware. To accomplish that, you must strengthen your mindfulness muscles through practice.

EXAMPLES OF MINDFULNESS EXERCISES

To practice mindfulness, you don't need any special equipment. You just need you, a little space, and some time.

DETAILED APPRECIATION

I'm starting with this exercise because it's something a lot of us—young and old—do less often. You don't know how significant a thing is until you pay attention to it. Think of the smallest thing that contributes to your daily activities. Pay attention to the benefits you get from that little thing. You'll realize that you've not given it the credit it deserves.

Most times, because we're used to seeing things work, we don't realize that some things or people make those things work.

The point of this exercise is to simply express gratitude for the seemingly insignificant things in life—those things that sustain your existence but rarely receive any consideration amid our desire for greater and better things.

For instance, electricity powers your iron; the postman delivers your mail. Your mouth allows you to take in food while your nose takes in the air, and your clothes keep you warm. However, do you know how these things and processes came to be or how they actually function? If they stop working, what do you think will happen?

Have you ever considered how life would be different without these things?

Have you ever stopped to consider the tiniest, tiniest details they have?

Have you ever taken some time to reflect on the connections that exist between these things and how, taken together, they contribute to the earth's overall operation?

To practice mindful appreciation,

> Identify three things you appreciate less yet are significant to your existence.

> Pay attention to their modalities and how they function. Your perspective about them will change.

CONSCIOUS WALKING

Mindful walking is the practice of becoming aware of your surroundings and how your body and mind feel while moving. Moving around can help some people become more aware of their bodies, minds, and the present moment.

Pick a route that lets you walk without interruption for at least ten minutes, preferably outside. Spend the time just walking. Don't do this when you're headed to a destination or running an errand.

1. Focus on your breathing while standing still for a few moments prior to beginning your walk. Keep track of how every part of your body is feeling.

2. Pay full attention to your body's movements and sensations as you begin to walk.

3. Pay attention to the sensations in your feet, legs, arms, chest, and head as you carry your body.

4. Start paying attention to the sights around you once you have connected with the sensations in your body.

5. Take note of how you feel when you are finished. Do you feel more focused, energized, or calm?

In Daphne's experience with mindful walking, it wasn't until about six months into the treatment that she personally believed the practice was beneficial. But before that, she almost gave up until one summer day when she was walking. During that walk, she naturally noticed that the trees around her were dropping leaves. She felt the warm sun on his face. When she realized this for the first time in years, she realized she had a life worth living. That was her Eureka moment.

INTENTIONAL EATING

When you eat intentionally, you use all your physical and emotional senses to enjoy and experience the foods you choose. This contributes to an increase in appreciation for food, which may enhance the eating experience as a whole.

You're encouraged to make choices about food that will satisfy and nourish the body through mindful eating. However, because eating experiences vary, it discourages judging your eating habits.

Therefore, mindful eating focuses on your eating experiences, body-related sensations, and thoughts and feelings about food with heightened awareness and without judgment.

Here's a simple model Fung et al. (2016) created to guide your mindfulness when eating:

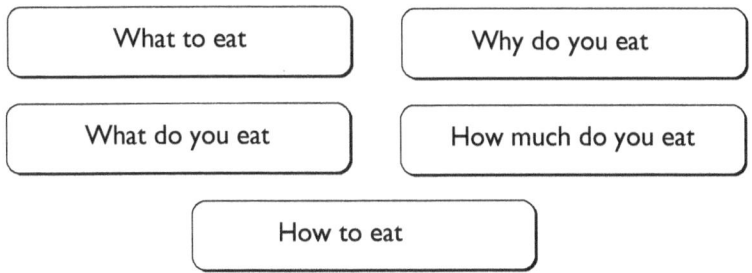

Hanh & Cheung (2010) suggest seven practices of mindful eating:

✓ **Respect the food.** Recognize who cooked the meal and where the food was grown. Eat without distractions to enhance the experience of eating.

✓ **Use every sense.** Take note of how you feel while eating as well as the sounds, colors, smells, tastes, and textures of the food. Take a break from time to time to use these senses.

✓ **Serve in small servings.** This may assist in preventing food waste and overeating. Fill only one dinner plate that is no bigger than nine inches across.

✓ **Enjoy each bite slowly and thoroughly.** The meal can be slowed down and the flavors of the food can be fully appreciated with these practices.

43

✓ **Eat slowly to avoid eating too much.** When you eat slowly, you are more likely to know when you are full and can stop eating, which is about **80%** of the time.

✓ **Avoid skipping meals.** When you go too long without eating, you run the risk of feeling a lot of hunger, which may cause you to choose the quickest and easiest food option, which isn't always healthy. These dangers can be reduced by planning meals for the same time each day and giving yourself enough time to eat or snack.

✓ **Eat a diet based on plants for your health and the environment.** Take into account the effects that certain foods have over time. Saturated fat and processed meat are linked to increased heart disease and colon cancer risk. The production of plant-based foods is less harmful to the environment than that of animal-based foods like meat and dairy.

Other mindful exercises you can practice include:

✓ Mindful Breathing

✓ Deliberate Listening

✓ Mindful Observation

✓ Mindful meditation

THE PURPOSE OF MINDFULNESS

Mindfulness serves a lot of purpose ...

FREEDOM FROM ANXIETY

One of the reasons we get worried is because we try to control something we don't have the power to—the future. Through mindfulness, you'll stop worrying about what will happen tomorrow or in years to come.

You'll begin to appreciate the blessings of today and now, and you'll live them to the fullest. A bright day today guarantees a bright future. Your "future" is a product of how you respond to today. Begin living in the present moment with awareness.

A TRANSITION FROM RESTLESSNESS TO REST

Restlessness isn't a good thing for a young mind. It could lead to some health challenges. Now, I'm sure you won't want to be a regular at the hospital.

Just like anxiety, restlessness takes away your peace. That's not good. You can only be happy and effective at what you do when you're at peace. Rest is a state of being at peace within, despite the situation outside.

Mindfulness brings you to the point where you're in the eye of a storm, unmoved and at peace. That's rest.

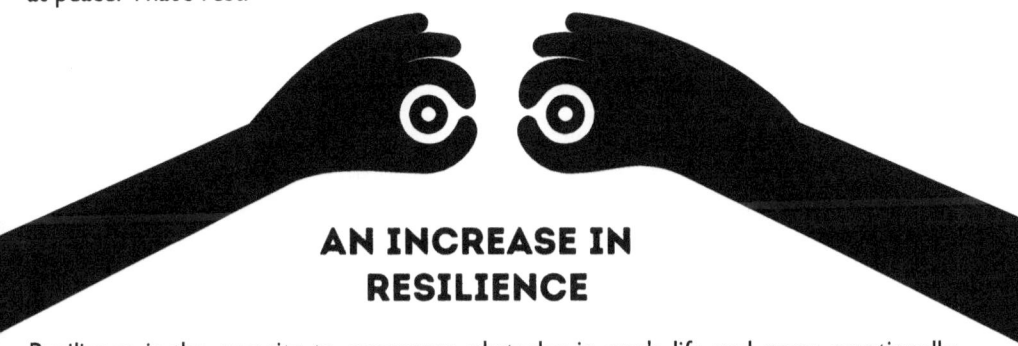

AN INCREASE IN RESILIENCE

Resilience is the capacity to overcome obstacles in one's life and grow emotionally, psychologically, and academically as a result. Training in mindfulness has been shown to help people build resilience and cultivate positive emotions and attitudes. Mindfulness-Based Cognitive Therapy is a specific therapy that aims to improve your social and emotional resilience while helping you identify and reduce "problem behaviors," attention issues, and anxiety.

REDUCED PAIN AND STRESS

This training teaches you to let go of pain and release stress. This is a scientifically proven method for reducing stress. The brain learns to accept and tolerate pain through mindfulness practice. You learn to treat pain as something that cannot be avoided rather than as a sign of danger.

It has been demonstrated that mindfulness-based stress reduction (MBSR) is just as effective as taking painkillers. In addition, the effect appears to last longer. Instead of using chemicals to combat pain, mindfulness teaches the brain to be more open to it.

BOOSTS PERFORMANCE

Are you into any sports? I've read many athletes vouch for mindfulness. The practice enhances their ability to focus and prevents distraction. Instead of stressing about the outcome, these athletes focus on the game's process and let the results take care of themselves.

Even if you are not an athlete, this mindfulness will enhance every part of your life45 academics, and relationships.

A REDUCTION IN SYMPTOMS OF DEPRESSION

Mindfulness has long been regarded as a successful treatment for depression. By assisting practitioners in identifying and taking a step back from intense negative emotions and feelings, it has been found to reduce depressive symptoms, anxiety, and stress levels. This idea of observing and letting go of thoughts and feelings rather than fighting them is the foundation of mindfulness.

1. NON-JUDGMENTAL

As you begin your mindfulness practice, you may begin to pay close attention to your thoughts. Avoid getting caught up in ideas, opinions, and preferences. Recognize that your mind has wandered and return it to your breath as soon as you notice it without judging yourself for not paying attention.

2. PATIENCE

Recognize and accept that things will unfold over time. Be open to each moment and patient with yourself. Instead of rushing to get somewhere else or better, give yourself permission to take the time you need for mindfulness and observe what is happening right now.

3. BEGINNER'S MIND

Try to see things clearly and without clutter. Too frequently, we allow our expectations, beliefs, and past experiences to prevent us from seeing things in the here and now.

As if you were experiencing something for the first time or seeing it through the eyes of a child, try opening yourself up to new possibilities.

4. TRUST

Trusting oneself and one's feelings is an essential component of meditation training. Despite the possibility of making mistakes along the way, trust your instincts and look within for direction. Learn to listen to and trust yourself while also being open to what you learn from others.

5. NON-STRIVING

Most of what you do in life probably has a goal or purpose. Mindfulness meditation, on the other hand, entails "non-doing" and concentrating on seeing and accepting things as they are right now. Try not to react or enter goal-setting mode. Embrace the present moment and maintain awareness.

6. ACCEPTANCE

Allowing things to be as they are without trying to change them is called acceptance. You can be more aware of what you are experiencing when you accept your current circumstance without wishing it were different or attempting to change it.

7. LETTING GO

As you begin to pay attention to your inner experiences during meditation, you may discover that your mind may want to hold onto particular thoughts or experiences. Try to let your experiences or thoughts be what they are. Try not to focus on how each experience should be judged. Simply allow it to be and let it go.

FINALLY ... PRACTICE! PRACTICE! PRACTICE!

Theresa practiced and internalized mindfulness to the point that she concluded she was in charge of her life, with herself in the driver's seat. She concluded that she didn't need to wait until her next treatment appointment to feel better. She had the resources she needed to deal with her emotions.

Just as lifting weights is necessary for weight training and picking up an instrument to play is important to learning it, practicing mindfulness is important to learning it.

Standing at the edge of a swimming pool to receive lessons on the techniques of swimming won't make you a swimmer. You have to get into the water and practice. So also, reading about mindfulness or listening to a podcast about it won't teach you any new skills. You must practice it.

Here's how I'll summarize everything I said in this chapter: to live a happy and fulfilling life, worry less about the past you can't alter and the future you can't control. Appreciate the present moment and live it to the fullest. You could do this while eating or walking mindfully.

Here's a simple question for you:

> How relevant is mindfulness to your experience?

CHAPTER 4: BUILDING RESILIENCE WITH DISTRESS TOLERANCE SKILLS

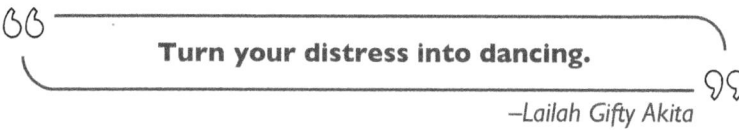

Turn your distress into dancing.

—Lailah Gifty Akita

Alice confessed that she regretted not seeking an ADHD diagnosis early enough and not confronting all her difficulties as a child. She couldn't blame herself for that because she knew nothing about it then. She was afraid of getting diagnosed because she didn't want to be judged. In her view, people tend to judge you when you're different. As a result, she had to internalize every emotion and endure every hardship until she could no longer bear it.

She was in her late 20s when she received a late diagnosis of ADHD during a session with a mental health professional. She knew she had those ADHD symptoms, but she didn't know that's what it was. She wished she had dealt with it earlier.

It can be challenging to control emotional stress, whether it's real or imagined. It's even worse if you don't know what you're dealing with. It'll result in more frustrations. And most ADHD patients have a short life span for frustration.

A person's capacity to manage actual or perceived emotional distress is known as *distress tolerance*. Every day, we all face various emotional challenges, ranging from minor irritations to high-stress situations. If you have distress tolerance, you can experience unpleasant and uncomfortable feelings without engaging in unhealthy behavior or worsening the situation.

In stressful situations, people with a low distress tolerance become overwhelmed and are more likely to use unhealthy coping mechanisms or have angry outbursts or meltdowns. This chapter aims to show you how one of the DBT skills—distress tolerance—can be used to curtail the emotional side of ADHD.

INTRODUCTION TO DISTRESS TOLERANCE SKILLS

Certain emotions may be brought on by attention deficit hyperactivity disorder (ADHD). For instance, you can feel guilty or humiliated about how you believe others view you. If your loved ones accuse you of not listening and you believe you have let them down in some manner, you could get anxious. Some other issues on the list below could also trigger intense emotions in ADHD patients:

- ✓ Having parents get divorced
- ✓ Getting into an argument with classmates,
- ✓ Receiving bullying,
- ✓ Not being cast in the role they desired for the school play
- ✓ High academic demands
- ✓ Failing an exam, etc.

But I want you to know that everyone else experiences the same feelings as you do. The only difference is that you could experience them longer or more powerfully due to ADHD, though. That doesn't make you a *weirdo*.

ADHD can indeed make you struggle to control your emotions, especially when it comes to strong emotions like anger, impatience, or sadness.

You're not from some extraterrestrial world, and you don't need some time on the lab table to understand yourself. Because I know that it hurts to feel intensely negative and have so little control over your responses. But *how bad could it be?* When others feel these emotions, emotional responsiveness can harm your social relationships.

Most teens with ADHD are impulsive people who just react depending on how urgent the circumstance is. If it's then coupled with adolescent shenanigans, it becomes unbearable. Does that apply to you?

However, did you know that by being able to wait before responding, you may respond more logically and somewhat detach yourself from your emotions? Sadly, I know this capacity to delay responding can occasionally be quite difficult for those with ADHD, at least the ones I've worked with.

I also know that some people with ADHD may just be more sensitive to criticism, recommendations, or even mild suggestions than others who didn't have ADHD growing up.

You can control those ADHD symptoms and emotions with the appropriate counseling and treatment. You can acquire new coping mechanisms and improve how you feel about living with ADHD.

The good news is that this is not an entirely hopeless situation. The frustration you feel as a result of your inability to control these emotional outbursts may lead you to believe you've reached a dead end, but this is not the case. Dr. Marsha Linehan came up with something learnable to put you in charge of your emotions instead of being at their mercy.

Linehan (cited by Compitus, 2020) believes that you can endure a sudden emotional crisis by having the ability to handle it without making it worse. That's one of the skills you'll learn in distress tolerance. When you feel out of control and powerless to change the circumstance, the distress tolerance skill will also assist you in accepting the truth of the scenario.

Another thing you'll learn through distress tolerance is how to manage your emotions when you're not sure what you need.

Emotional stress could pose a real-time crisis, but this DBT skill is up to the task. It's designed to help you survive this crisis.

WHAT ELSE DO YOU NEED TO KNOW ABOUT DISTRESS TOLERANCE?

Generally, the founding principle in DBT is acceptance and change. Do you remember this from the previous chapters?

Now, one of the first orientations you'll get when learning distress tolerance skills is that it's not only acceptable to experience feelings of sadness or anxiety but that it's also crucial to acquire the ability to accept them. Then you'll learn how to tolerate pain and distress skillfully. Therefore, you'll learn to recognize and accept emotions in a non-judgmental way rather than becoming overwhelmed by them or hiding from them, avoiding unhealthy or self-destructive choices.

Don't think that with these skills, your emotions will change. No, you'll still get angry, you'll still feel sad, and you'll still feel disappointed even after learning this skill. The only difference you'll notice after acquiring distress tolerance skills is how to respond better to your emotions. Your response is what will, essentially, make the difference. Therefore, don't struggle to change your emotions because that's not the objective of this skill.

WHAT ARE THE DISTRESS TOLERANCE SKILLS THAT WE CAN LEARN?

The following distress tolerance skills are taught most frequently:

- Self-Soothe
- TIPP
- IMPROVE the moment
- ACCEPTS

These skills are often tagged "*crisis survival skills*" because they assist a person in traversing a perceived or actual crisis. The fact about human beings is that none of us really finds it pleasurable to go through pain or anything that causes discomfort. We often try to find ways to avoid those pains or get rid of them. That is what drives us to seek ways to alleviate the pain.

Mckay et al. (cited by Compitus, 2020) said that self-harm behaviors—cutting, burning, etc.—are examples of ways some people numb pain. Using alcohol or drugs, running away from the situation, or denying that the pain exists are other options some people choose. According to Mckay and his colleagues, numbing emotional pain doesn't eventually take the pain away; rather, it causes more harmful behavioral patterns with serious long-term consequences.

However, the crisis survival skills I listed above are short-term coping mechanisms that can help you better manage your emotional pains and prevent destructive behavioral patterns. You'll get to learn more about these skills in the next session. You're in safe hands (smile).

HOW TO BUILD DISTRESS TOLERANCE SKILLS AND HOW TO USE THEM

Before I start to show you more about each of these distress tolerance skills, I need you to understand this. You're unique and different from everyone else. These skills don't work the same for everyone because of our uniqueness. Therefore, I'll need you to do two things in this session:

✓ Pay rapt attention to how each skill works

✓ Test to see which skills are best suited to you.

Are we cool with that?

1. SELF-SOOTHE

It is generally believed that the capacity to self-soothe develops during early childhood through the internalization of reassuring experiences. Have you ever seen a child sucking their thumb or stroking a stuffed animal? Those are examples of self-soothing techniques some children naturally develop.

But if you didn't, you can still learn these skills through deliberate strategies. Learning these strategies could be difficult for some people, though. Those natural self-soothing abilities children develop can also be adapted for teens and young adults.

52

ARE YOU WONDERING HOW THOSE SELF-SOOTHING SKILLS CAN BE ADAPTED FOR TEENS?

Well, that's the whole point of learning.

Here's an explanation of why self-soothing should be adapted to help you control your emotions. Usually, our (human beings') emotional brain takes over when we're emotionally stimulated. When this happens, our natural instinct is to do something that could be harmful to ourselves or others. During those times, the rational part of the brain is offline.

In order to regain control over your actions at that moment, you must first calm your emotional brain. Self-soothing can help accomplish this. Instead of doing something harmful or likely to worsen things, you can do something else that brings you joy and comfort.

According to Schwartz (2022), engaging in activities that are relaxing, reassuring, and centered on the five senses to relieve stress is known as "self-soothing." Below are examples of how you can engage your five senses:

SIGHT

✓ If you're close to a park during the emotional distress, focus on the beautiful way the sky, trees, grass, benches, and people create a collage of colors and life in nature. If you're not, just focus on the scenery around you.

✓ Go for art or pictures!

✓ You could turn your attention to a movie that helps you relax.

✓ For subsequent occurrences, you could create a collection of pictures that make you happy and help you relax. Whenever you feel emotionally distressed, you can flip through those pictures.

HEARING

✓ Instead of expressing your emotional stress immediately, you could turn to someone you like and whose voice makes you happy. This could be through a phone call or a social media platform.

✓ Music—good and calm music—could also do the trick. Listening to one could calm you. So instead of an outburst of rage, take out your mobile device, plug your ear pod into your ears, and play the music.

✓ You could also turn your attention to the lively sounds around you—birds, wind, and people talking. One of the best places to get this combo is at a park.

- ✓ If you play a musical instrument, that's even better. Pour out your emotions while you play alone.
- ✓ Listening to your favorite audiobook or podcast at that time isn't a bad option either.

SMELL

- ✓ Before leaving your room, you could put on a cologne or perfume you like to smell.
- ✓ You could transfer your energy into preparing a meal that smells good.

  Flowers! If you love them, you could purchase and keep them fresh in your room.

- ✓ You could sneak to a place to enjoy the scent of a bakery, flower shop, perfume shop, or restaurant.

TASTE

- ✓ You could escape to an eatery to buy your favorite meal at your favorite restaurant. Or even order it online.
- ✓ You could choose to buy some snacks or comfort foods. A caution here: eat moderately.
- ✓ Make yourself a cup of cocoa, coffee, tea, or any other beverage you like. Alcohol is a no!
- ✓ You could chew or blow some gum while chewing.

TOUCH

- ✓ Hold your pet in your lap and pet it.
- ✓ You could wrap yourself in your favorite clothes. Take pleasure in the way they feel on your skin.
- ✓ You could take a shower and relax in the warm, calming water. If that suits you better, you can also take a cold shower.
- ✓ You can go for a massage or massage yourself, as the case may be.
- ✓ Touch something silky, supple, or fluffy.

Rather than remaining in a crisis, opt for self-soothing. It is less stressful. You can choose which of the senses works best for you.

2. TIPP

TIPP is another distress tolerance skill. It's an acronym for:

T – Temperature

I – Intense exercise,

P – Paced breathing

P – Paired muscle relaxation.

TEMPERATURE

Our bodies frequently become hot when we are upset. Altering your body temperature could help you change your mood quickly and keep you from doing something rash. To combat this, you could:

Splash some cold water on your face

Put a cold ice pack on your face or hold an ice cube

Turn on air conditioning in your room or an alternative to blow on your face.

INTENSE EXERCISE

Stress levels go down when oxygen flow is increased, and it's hard to hold on to explosive emotions when you're physically exhausted and out of breath. So,

✓ Run! Sprint to the end of the street

✓ Punch some punchbag hard. Or exercise hard to match your intense feelings.

✓ Jump in the pool for a few laps or do jumping jacks until you get tired

Additionally, when you're tired, it's hard to stay dangerously upset.

RHYTHMIC BREATHING

In case you didn't know, breathing exercises can reduce stress levels. It reduces emotional pain. You can try these breathing exercises:

Box/square breathing:
While tracing the four lines of a square, hold your breath for four counts and let go of your breath for four counts. Repeat until you feel more at ease.

Nose-mouth breathing:
Try inhaling through your nose for seven seconds and exhaling through your mouth for ten.

4-4-8 breathing:
First inhale through your nose for four counts, hold your breath for another four counts, then exhale for eight counts. When you exhale, purse your lips to hear your breath coming out.

This type of breathing manipulation causes your heart rate to slow.

PAIRED MUSCLE RELAXATION

Teens with ADHD are usually tense, sometimes without knowing it. Paired muscle relaxation works like this:

✓ First, tighten a single muscle or group of muscles very strongly.

✓ Hold that position for ten seconds.

✓ Then, relax the muscle.

Your heart rate and breathing will slow down as your muscles relax and require less oxygen.

Sokya (2021) suggested that to practice paired muscle relaxation, any of the following muscle groups can be targeted:

✓ Make fists with your hands and arms,

✓ Make fists and tense your biceps and triceps,

✓ Wrinkle your forehead,

- ✓ Close your eyelids tightly.

- ✓ Push your chin down toward your chest.

- ✓ Take a deep breath and hold it – this is for your chest.

- ✓ Tense your stomach muscles.

- ✓ Squeeze your buttocks and gluts together.

- ✓ Point your toes down.

3. IMPROVE THE MOMENT

Greene (2020) said that improving the moment helps us get through emotionally challenging situations when a technique like self-soothing isn't working. The DBT IMPROVE the Moment skills are meant to provide you with options you can choose from when faced with an emotionally challenging circumstance. You don't need to practice them all.

The goal of the IMPROVE skill is to make the moment more pleasant and bearable by substituting a more positive action for the immediate event that sparked negative feelings.

IMPROVE is an acronym for

I – Imagery
M – Meaning
P – Prayer
R – Relaxation
O – One thing right now
V – Vacation
E – Encouragement

IMAGERY

This technique requires you to put your mind to work to achieve emotional de-stress. There are a few applications for this ability:

- ✓ Picture yourself in a completely secure location with everything you require.

- ✓ Picture yourself overcoming the difficult situation you're in right now.

- ✓ Imagine that you are releasing hurtful feelings.

Engage your mind to create an emotionally stable world for yourself.

MEANING

Have you realized that, sometimes, certain things just happen to you that aren't your fault? The truth is that some painful situations can sometimes have a deeper meaning for us if we look beyond the pain. Try to find meaning in difficult circumstances. What can that experience teach you? You might become more sympathetic. You might form new relationships. You might begin your healing journey with this. Find a reason because there's one.

PRAYER

This is not about a specific religion. Everyone prays, in a way. But prayer has a different outlook for different people. It could be giving things over to a higher power or connecting with a wise mind. This approach takes you beyond yourself to seek help from someone or something greater than yourself.

RELAXATION

Our instinct to fight or flight makes us tense up in stressful situations. To alleviate the mental pain, try engaging in activities that can calm you. As an example, consider:

- ✓ Yoga
- ✓ Hot/cold bath
- ✓ Taking a long walk
- ✓ Deep breathing, etc.

ONE THING IN THE MOMENT

Did you remember the skill of mindfulness? This technique is similar to it. Let go of the future and the past to stay in the present. To solve the issue, it will not be helpful to bring up old issues or to speculate about what might happen in the future. Concentrate entirely on completing a single task. Emotions are less overwhelming when the mind is focused in one direction.

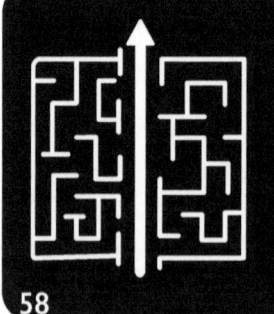

VACATION

C'mon! You need a break! We all take breaks from time to time. This technique says you should give yourself a break, provided it doesn't lead to additional issues. The "vacation" shouldn't be long, just a few hours. This may require you to go back to bed or turn off your phone for a day. Sometimes you just need to watch a show on TV for a few hours. You should determine how your vacation will look.

ENCOURAGEMENT

I love this the most. This technique asks you to assume a new role—that of a cheerleader. For which team? Team You! You need to learn to cheer yourself on more often. If you tend to be critical of yourself, it's time to begin to see that you're worth more. Tell yourself,

"I can get through this."

"I'm trying my hardest."

"This is difficult, but it will pass."

It may be difficult initially, but you need to.
You want to hear *you*.

4. ACCEPTS

ACCEPTS is a distraction skill. It's designed to distract you from difficult emotional situations and help you get through those emotional situations one moment at a time.

ACCEPTS is a set of skills that are part of the DBT distress tolerance model to help you tolerate negative emotions until you can address and ultimately resolve the situation. So, while you're in emotional distress, and you don't want to act based on how you feel, ACCEPTS says you should:

A – engage in some productive **ACTIVITIES** like volunteering.

C – **CONTRIBUTE** to the well-being of someone else, or to a cause. You could contribute to a project or cook with someone. Help a friend or family member.

C – **COMPARE** your present situation with a worse situation you've experienced before or with someone else's situation. You could read about people going through difficult times.

E – switch your **EMOTIONS**. Watch a comic animation, listen to music, or watch a funny clip.

P – **PUSH AWAY** the situation from your mind by leaving it for a while.

T – redirect your **THOUGHTS**. You could play a game, count something, read a book, or just do anything that takes your thoughts somewhere, but the emotional situation is different.

S – as in "self-soothe," means to create positive **SENSATIONS** using your five senses to relieve you of stress.

Some other distress tolerance skills include:

PROS AND CONS

Most times when we're overwhelmed by emotions, we become impulsive, and our logical side goes offline. Such impulsiveness is heightened in people with ADHD. However, the essence of this skill is to help you put logic over emotions. Pros and Cons simply teaches you to consider the good and bad sides of the action you're about to take before you act on it. Ask yourself:

- ✓ What is the effectiveness of the behavior now and in the future?

- ✓ Is the behavior harmful or incompatible with your objectives?

- ✓ What are the benefits and drawbacks of engaging in crisis behavior or acting on your impulses?

- ✓ Before a recurring impulsive reaction occurs, you can answer these questions beforehand, write them on a plain sheet of paper or in your journal, and take it with you as a reminder.

RADICAL ACCEPTANCE

The complete and utter acceptance of reality is radical acceptance. This indicates that your mind, heart, and body accept the situation as it is. You accept reality instead of fighting against it.

DBT distress tolerance skills focus on tolerating one's emotions during painful events, reducing impulsive behavior in a crisis, and accepting the situation as it is without trying to change it.

WHAT ELSE CAN YOU DO TO COPE WITH STRESS?

Don't forget that no one skill fits all here. Because of our uniqueness, there are specific skills that suit each of us. You deserve to have lots of options you could try before settling on a few you know will work for you.

After you've learned and practiced those distress skills, here are three things you can

REDEFINE WHO YOU ARE

Who do you want to be known as? An impulsive individual with no emotional control? Will you continue to allow your emotions to define who you are? You're better than your emotions.

Redefine who you are, and then let your emotions align with that definition. If your emotions attempt to run wild, use any coping skills to control them. Ultimately, knowing who you are can help you tolerate emotional distress.

RECOVER YOUR IMAGE

Wouldn't it be nice to hear someone say, "I thought you would yell at me, but you didn't?" That's new …" It sounds like someone is recovering their image. No one should label you based on your negative emotional reactions. There's a better version of you.

You won't want to ruin an image you're trying to build with another act of emotional outburst, would you?

REDISCOVER YOUR CORE VALUES

Your values are the norms, morals, principles, and ideals that give your life meaning, value, and significance. Those are the things that give you reasons to get out of bed in the morning and the drive to keep going. You can begin to build a life that is worth living by discovering or rediscovering your values. This will help you tolerate emotional distress.

A recap of the lessons in this chapter: you'll handle issues better if you can learn to manage distress. This skill gives you various tools you can adopt to achieve this. You can engage your human senses to distract you from an annoying situation. You could IMPROVE, and you can also burn your anger through intense exercise.

Most importantly, redefining who you are, what you want to be known for, and what you stand for could also shape your responses to situations.

There are still more things to learn in this book on how to cope with ADHD using DBT. But before you proceed, attempt these questions:

How can you apply any of the distress tolerance skills to a practical issue you've faced before?

Which of the skills is most fitting for you?

CHAPTER 5: EMOTIONAL REGULATION SKILLS: PAYING ATTENTION TO YOUR FEELINGS

> 66 In between every action and reaction, there is a space. Usually the space is extremely small because we react so quickly, but take notice of that space and expand it. Be aware in that space that you have a choice to make. You can choose how to respond ... 99

— *Rebecca Eanes*

INTRODUCTION TO EMOTIONAL REGULATION SKILLS

Theo was a fifth-grader when he started to receive his behavioral healthcare at school. His mother realized that Theo had been through a lot, including losing a loved one. Those events began to wear on him emotionally. He struggled emotionally and with some behaviors. Theo got angry and anxious more often.

When Theo was diagnosed, it was discovered that ADHD was the cause of his anger outbursts and impulsiveness. By applying emotional regulation skills, Theo began to learn self-control. He became aware of his anger and how to feel it healthily. Whenever he noticed difficulty sitting still or paying attention in class, he spoke with his teacher about it.

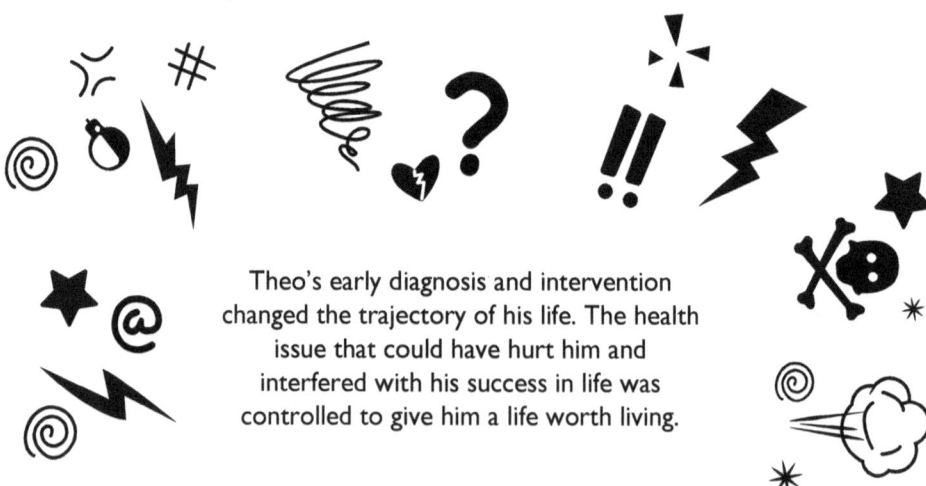

Theo's early diagnosis and intervention changed the trajectory of his life. The health issue that could have hurt him and interfered with his success in life was controlled to give him a life worth living.

EMOTIONS AND THE PECULIARITY OF YOUR AGE

Adolescents have a harder time controlling their emotions because they frequently get into fights with their parents and peers. Adolescents with ADHD are especially vulnerable to this.

Teens with ADHD have a lot of trouble controlling their negative emotions, but many also have trouble controlling their positive emotions. Specifically, adolescents with ADHD frequently exhibit age-inappropriate levels of enthusiasm or exuberance when they are happy or excited. When they hear good news, they might scream, jump up and down, and invade other people's personal space. As a result, these teenagers are frequently viewed as immature and brash by peers, teachers, and family.

Breaux (2020) said that people in your age group who have ADHD exhibit rapid and drastic emotional shifts, stronger responses to stress or frustration, and intense displays of both positive and negative emotions.

Also, Littman (2022) said that a significant and overwhelming period of change occurs when you're a preteen or a teen. Teens with ADHD have trouble navigating the following:

✓ A need for sensitivity to peer acceptance, a growing social life, questions about identity, and a desire for independence.

✓ Changes in the body and the development of sexuality which frequently cause embarrassment and confusion.

✓ Mood swings and more emotionality which are caused by hormonal changes. Girls' ADHD symptoms are intensified by monthly drops in estrogen levels during puberty.

✓ Stress is caused by increased academic demands and frequently decreased parental support.

BUT HAVE YOU EVER WONDERED WHAT EMOTIONS ARE?

Dr. Bruce Lipton (cited by DBT Tools, n.d.) said that emotions arise in response to a stimulus. A thought, a sound, a smell, or a sight can all act as triggers. Emotions and thoughts result from triggers. We are motivated to take action as soon as the emotion occurs.

> Good news! We can learn to regulate our emotions and how we react to things.

SO, WHAT IS EMOTION REGULATION?

Emotional regulation is one of the skills you'll learn under dialectical behavior therapy (DBT). I mentioned this to you in a previous chapter.

Taking any action that changes the intensity of an emotional experience is what emotional regulation is. This skill doesn't teach you to avoid or suppress what you feel. Rather, it teaches you to control it. Thus, you can control the emotions you experience and how you express them.

The goal of the emotional regulation skill is to enable you to:

✓ Comprehend the function of emotions

✓ Understand the urge that goes along with each emotion

✓ Make the decision to heed or resist these urges.

✓ Reduce vulnerability

✓ Build resilience against negative emotions

✓ Improve your mental health as a whole.

The emotional regulation skills you need to learn are:

✓ STOP   ✓ PLEASE

✓ Opposite Action   ✓ Build Mastery

✓ ABC   ✓ Positive Self-Talk

We'll talk more about this later in this chapter.

WHY IS EMOTIONAL REGULATION IMPORTANT?

You can better deal with stress, interact with others, and focus on learning when you learn how to control your emotions. Instead of suppressing your emotions, many experts believe it's essential for teens to learn how to manage their feelings.

Learning how to control your emotions has lots of benefits. A teen with ADHD will benefit more from it.

MORE DELIBERATE IN DECISION-MAKING

Think about coming home after a challenging day at school to spend time with your family. It's so easy to enter the house or the next room and lash out at others, but you can't. Do you know why? It's like you have no control over it since it simply happens.

Life doesn't have to seem chaotic. Instead of letting your emotions control your conduct, you may choose how you want to act on purpose. Once you have improved your emotional regulation, you can make deliberate decisions in situations rather than simply reacting. This can help you feel less out of control and more in control of your life.

FREEDOM TO MAKE HEALTHY CHOICES

The worst moment to make a decision is when we're emotionally unbalanced. During that time, we make some poor decisions. Some young adults make bad decisions on food, leisure time, or interpersonal relationships during such moments. And instead of getting better, a feeling of emptiness and dissatisfaction follows. It further intensifies the emotional distress.

The ability to control your emotions doesn't guarantee you won't make the same choices or decisions. What it really implies is that you'll have a choice between what is good and bad for you. You're free to decide what's healthy for you and what isn't.

HEALTHY COMMUNICATION

Did you know that communication is the soul of any relationship? Have you tried talking back to someone when you're upset? What happened to your relationship with that person afterward?

You will not express your wants or desires to others intelligently if you are emotionally unbalanced. It'll result in a breakdown in your relationship with others.

Your relationships with others will be better if you learn to regulate your emotions. You'll be able to listen properly and convey your messages better with your emotions under control.

PEACEFUL RELATIONSHIP

Healthy communication will produce a peaceful relationship. It's only when you're calm that you can express concern for someone else.

When you speak with your peers and colleagues at school with controlled emotion, you will be at ease with them. People keep their distance from anyone who speaks to them rashly.

A SENSE OF FULFILLMENT

When you're able to develop a healthy relationship that gives you peace and you can make healthy, wise choices for yourself, it gives you a sense of satisfaction and fulfillment. You'll be pleased with yourself for doing the right thing for yourself.

IMPROVED SELF-ESTEEM

An emotionally distressed teen will always think less of themselves. They'll not see anything good about themselves, so it'll be difficult to speak confidently with others without looking down.

They're usually critical of themselves. Emotional regulation skills will help you accept and embrace yourself without being critical of your flaws. Overall, it'll boost your self-esteem and confidence. You'll learn to appreciate yourself more and acknowledge your worth and strengths instead of focusing on your weaknesses.

RECOGNIZING AND COPING WITH STRONG EMOTIONS

How are you feeling right now?

Are you interested in what I've been sharing?

Are you hopeful that you'll get to know who you are?

Are you happy because it's a school project you enjoy or bored because this is something you must do for school and you don't really enjoy it?

Something else may distract you, such as getting excited about your weekend plans or being sad because you just broke up with someone.

According to *KidsHealth Behavioral Health* experts, these feelings are normal for people. They inform us of what we are going through and assist us in determining how to respond.

The ability to recognize what we're feeling and put it into words rather than just reacting in a childlike manner is known as *emotional awareness*. Emotional awareness is simply recognizing, valuing, and accepting your emotions as they arise. We become better at understanding why and what we are feeling with practice and time.

Before you can cope with or control your emotions, you need to recognize them first.

SO, HOW DO YOU RECOGNIZE YOUR EMOTIONS?

#1 - IDENTIFY AND ADMIT THE EMOTION

Identifying your current emotion is the first step. It takes practice to learn to notice and identify your emotions. But it's possible. So here's what you can do:

- ✓ Pick just one emotion if you're feeling more than one.
- ✓ Sit down for a moment and pay attention to your thoughts and physical sensations if you are having trouble identifying the emotion.
- ✓ Try to give an emotion you're experiencing a name (such as sadness, rage, or shame) if you can. For instance:

    I'm so *mad* at that Jeff in my study group!

    I feel *scared* every time I'm called to give a presentation.

- ✓ Make a note of the emotion on a slip of paper once you have given it a name.

✓ Don't conceal/suppress your feelings from yourself.

✓ Know the reasons behind your emotions. Determine what caused you to feel the way you do. For instance:

> Jeff always gets credit for other people's efforts.

✓ Don't blame anyone for your emotions once you've recognized them.

✓ Don't judge yourself for feeling the way you do. Consider it a normal thing. Acknowledging how you feel can help you move on. So, don't be hard on yourself.

#2 - ACT!

You can decide whether you need to express your feelings after you've identified them. Acknowledging them could be enough at times, but at other times, acting could make you feel better.

✓ How best can you express what you feel? Do you need to gently confront someone who infuriated you? Or discuss your feelings with a friend? Or go for a run to get rid of the emotion? Thinking this through makes you a master over your emotions. That's the essence of this skill.

✓ Find a way to alter your mood. You will need to learn how to transform your negative mood into a positive one at some point. Otherwise, your thoughts might become stuck on how bad things are, which could make you feel worse.

✓ Consciously develop positive feelings. Focus regularly on the good things in your life, even the little things. Being mindful of what's good about a situation switches your mood from negativity to positivity—pessimism to optimism.

✓ Talk to someone about how you feel.

✓ Exercise is helpful, too. Physical exercises release stress and help the brain to produce chemicals that promote a positive mood.

#3 - AVOID TRIGGERS

Triggers are things that others say or do to influence us and draw a reaction from us. You might know or have people like that around you. They're just good at saying or doing things to manipulate or disorient you until they get a furious response from you.

They usually strike you in sensitive areas on purpose to incite you to rage. Such action makes you vulnerable to them. What do you do?

- ✓ Resolve that no one has the right to determine how you feel, regardless of what they say or do to you. When you grant them that right, they will believe they control you and will make you dance to their music.

- ✓ Forgive yourself. Some people might be using something in your past to incite you to anger. When you forgive yourself and start living in the moment, such talks will not hold any weight against you.

- ✓ Rely on your judgment, not other people's judgment of things.

- ✓ Avoid blaming yourself. You're not to blame for someone else's inability to take responsibility for their lives. Don't let anyone make you feel guilty.

- ✓ Such people are toxic; avoid them. Draw a boundary to keep them away. Stay away from people who project their negative experiences on you. They're toxic people.

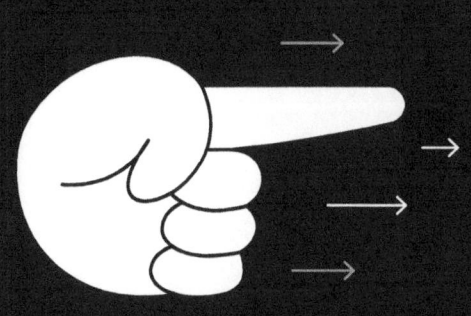

#4 - DON'T ISOLATE YOURSELF

Negative thoughts thrive the most when we're alone. And once you open your mind to a single thread of thought, it begins to grow until you're compelled to act on it. Those thoughts result in difficult emotions that persist for days and become difficult to shake off no matter what you do.

In this instance,

- ✓ Defy shame and open up to a friend, a family member, or your teacher, as the case may be.

- ✓ Instead of opting to act on the emotions, step out of your cocoon and seek help from an older person you can trust or a specialist.

SIX MOST USEFUL EMOTION REGULATION SKILLS YOU SHOULD MASTER

I mentioned those skills while introducing this DBT technique. Let's begin to talk about them one after the other here:

STOP

Greene (2020) refers to this as an "emergency mindfulness skill." Just imagine what the STOP traffic sign on our roads does to drivers. It's a regulatory sign that brings them to a complete halt, right? They're not to proceed until the intersection is clear of vehicles.

The STOP traffic sign has been adapted as an essential DBT skill to regulate your emotions.

S – Stop!

Simply stop! Whenever you think your feelings are in charge, stop! Don't respond. Simply freeze, particularly the mouth muscles. You can avoid doing what your emotions want you to do (act without thinking) by temporarily not drawing any conclusions until you have gathered enough facts to guide your decision.

P – Proceed mindfully

This is the part where you get to act based on the facts you've gathered on the issue. At this point, you would have thought through the best outcome in that situation. Then you act on it.

OPPOSITE ACTION

This skill teaches you to do the exact opposite of your emotion. Sounds difficult? Yeah, I know, but it's also practicable. Here's the trick:

✓ Instead of getting *angry*, show kindness, concern or just walk away

✓ Instead of feeling *ashamed*, raise your head high and your shoulders back and advance

✓ Instead of being *afraid*, muster courage within, match forward, and remain involved.

However, don't do the exact opposite when you're faced with danger. Fear grips you when you're faced with danger. It's wise to respond to the flight mode and save yourself from harm.

ABC

This skill teaches you to

> **A** – Accumulate positive emotions by engaging in activities that give you positive emotions.

> **B** – Build mastery by engaging in activities that you enjoy. It could be domestic skills or games.

> **C** – Cope ahead by preparing for those things that make you anxious or fidget. Prepare for that class presentation, test, or exam ahead.

PLEASE

According to Dr. Paul Greene (cited by Rigby, n. d.), although it may seem counterintuitive, some of the best things we can do to control our emotions take place well before they occur. This especially has to do with how we take care of our bodies.

Hence, to learn this skill, you need to remember that your mind affects your body and vice versa.

Dr. Greene cautions ahead that these skills might look simple, but we've often neglected at least one of them when our emotions get the best of us.

PL – Physical illness. There's a link between your physical and mental health. Emotional regulation becomes difficult if you're not physically sound. Take care of your physical health, and you will have also taken care of your mind.

E – Eat a healthy, balanced diet regularly. Skipping meals can affect your mental health.

A – Avoid drugs or substances that alter your mood.

S – Sleep well every night. It's essential to your health and well-being.

E – Exercising your body for about 20 minutes daily is good for your mental and physical fitness.

If you want to opt for this skill, ask yourself, "How well have I been faring with these practices?"

BUILD MASTERY

Just as in ABC skills, engage in an activity that gives you pleasure.

- ✓ Devote time to learn as much as you can on that thing.
- ✓ Talk about what you're learning with someone else, perhaps someone who knows it better.
- ✓ Practice, practice, and practice some more till you feel competent.

You can as well:

- ✓ Try something new
- ✓ Practice until you gain some level of competence
- ✓ Don't hesitate to give yourself credit for each progress you make

AFFIRMATIVE SELF-TALK

PsychCentral suggests five ways you can practice affirmative self-talk:

1. Pay attention to what your inner critic is saying about you to you.

2. Create a psychological distance from yourself.

3. If the conversation isn't lifting you, change the conversation to agree with your worth, essence, and youSpeak compassionately to yourself as you would to a friend.

4. Instead of saying "I Can't" to resist the urge to express a negative emotion, say "I Don't." For instance:

    "I can't miss my homework" against "I don't miss my homework."

    "I can't get angry" against "I don't get angry."

    "I can't hit a colleague" against "I don't hit a colleague."

According to Vanessa Patrick (cited by PsychCentral, 2015), saying "I don't" puts you in charge of your emotions.r goals. You shouldn't be talking down yourself.

WHAT IS EMOTIONAL REGULATION DISORDER?

We wouldn't need to regulate our emotions if there hadn't been a form of dysregulation. Did you catch my drift?

So let's talk about emotional regulation disorder, but you can also call it emotional dysregulation.

Cuncic (2022) described emotional dysregulation as a poorly regulated emotional response that falls outside a range of commonly accepted emotional responses. This could be significant mood swings, mood changes, or lability. Examples of dysregulation include sadness, rage, irritability, and frustration.

Teens with emotional dysregulation experience volatile, uncontrollable, and explosive feelings, which is one of the most impairing symptoms of ADHD.

DO YOU STILL REMEMBER SOMETHING ABOUT THE PECULIARITIES OF YOUR AGE?

Those are the years full of a never-ending series of highs and lows. It's usually a rapid, difficult, and frequent transition between euphoria and misery, jealousy and generosity, irritability and vulnerability. These transitions hit differently for teenagers who suffer from ADHD. It's also associated with emotional dysregulation.

EMOTIONAL DYSREGULATION AND SOCIAL MEDIA

Did you know that emotional dysregulation affects every aspect of your adolescent life? That includes your friendships, romantic relationships, academic performance, and even the use of social media. That's a whole lot of stress to deal with.

Even though social media is a cool place to be and meet new people who are netizens, *The Wall Street Journal* reported that the use of social media, specifically Instagram, was linked to poor mental health outcomes for teen girls, who cited body image issues and even suicidal thoughts in a 2021 research study. This is particularly troubling.

Social media could also have a real negative effect on teens' mental health. Are you aware of issues like cyberbullying, extremism, sexual and financial manipulation, and addiction resulting from an excessive reliance on online relationships?

Teens with emotional dysregulation may be particularly vulnerable to these risks and effects of social media use because they are already more sensitive to peer rejection and acceptance than their neurotypical peers.

WHAT CAUSES IT?

There might be numerous answers to this, but according to Cuncic (2022), one of the clear ones is the one that comes from an early psychological trauma inflicted by a caregiver's abuse or neglect. And it could lead to a condition known as "reactive attachment disorder."

Another probable cause is when one is raised by a parent with emotional dysregulation.

WHAT ARE ITS SYMPTOMS?

Emotional dysregulation can manifest in adolescents with ADHD in the following ways:

- ✓ Impulsivity in emotions
- ✓ Low tolerance for frustration
- ✓ Quick to get angry
- ✓ Inability to cope with stress
- ✓ Avoidance of difficult circumstances
- ✓ Overwhelmed by emotions

- ✓ Mood swings
- ✓ Defensiveness
- ✓ Verbal and physical violence
- ✓ Anxiety
- ✓ Depression
- ✓ Intense emotions

WHAT ARE THE EFFECTS OF EMOTIONAL DYSREGULATION FOR A TEEN SUFFERING FROM ADHD?

The following outcomes may occur:

- ✓ Likely to be defiant
- ✓ Issues with complying with requests from teachers or parents
- ✓ Sensitivity to depression
- ✓ Explosive relationships with family and peers
- ✓ Issues with making and maintaining friends
- ✓ Limited focus on tasks
- ✓ Risky sexual behavior
- ✓ Self-harm

HOW TO MANAGE EMOTIONS WHEN YOU HAVE ADHD

The answer to this is the emotional regulation skills I shared with you in this chapter. I recommend you go over them again and start practicing with anyone appropriate for you. That's how to manage your emotions as a teen with ADHD.

Remember, you're the boss of your emotions. Take charge with these skills.

Let's do a quick recap - this chapter made having healthy relationships look possible despite your emotional instability and outbursts. With the different tools and practical tools shared in this chapter like STOP, ABC, and PLEASE, you can regulate your emotions.

It's important for you also to remember that emotions are neither good nor bad; your response to how you feel labels the emotion good or bad. You can regulate your emotions without hurting anyone, or yourself, using the skills listed in this chapter.

What are the causes of emotional dysregulation you know?

What are the things that trigger emotional outburst in you?

Which emotional regulation skill works best for you?

CHAPTER 6: MANAGING INTENSE AND RAGING EMOTIONS WITH DBT

66 Anger is just anger. It isn't good. It isn't bad. It just is. What you do with it is what matters. It's like anything else. You can use it to build or to destroy. You just have to make the choice. 99

— Jim Butcher

Saline (2021) once shared the case of a frantic parent who reported that her 15-year-old teenage son's anger frightened her. She said her son used to take Focalin XR since he had been diagnosed with ADHD. Whenever they disagreed about his social life, he got angry. He has gotten enraged to the extent of kicking a hole in his bedroom door. She said whenever they argue, he verbally abuses her by calling her X-rated names. She solicited help because, obviously, she had lost it with the kid.

Can I ask you this?

"How intense are your emotions?"

"Do you get so angry that your parents become afraid of you?"

"How bad does it get?"

Now, I didn't ask those questions to make you feel bad. It's just a simple way of diagnosing your situation. You don't have to judge yourself because I'm not sitting in the judgment seat either. So, attempt those questions again.

While she was trying to respond to the frantic parent's concern, Saline (2021) stated that teens with ADHD can become enraged due to fluctuating hormone levels and poor working memory, and parents frequently bear the brunt of this. Knowing this may not make dealing with your teen's raging outbursts any easier.

Wexelblatt (2022) also shared the story of another teenager with an intense anger issue. The teenage boy was called Daniel. He was a landmine because he was silent and alone until a family member stepped in the wrong direction. He immediately explodes at that point. The most horrifying error made by Daniel's parents was denying him unlimited screen time. 14-year-old Daniel would scream at his parents and younger siblings when they restricted his video game play. Additionally, he would move toward his parents as if he were going to hit them and make suicidal threats.

Daniel was unable to alter his behavior despite seeing several therapists. It got worse in middle school.

INTRODUCTION: THE CONNECTION BETWEEN ANGER AND ADHD

Don't you want to know the mystery behind your intense rage? Let's start with that.

Ohwovoriole (2021) described anger as that intense emotion when something goes wrong or someone wrongs you. Typically, it's characterized by feelings of stress, annoyance, and resentment.

Before going further, it's crucial to inform you that we all get angry occasionally. It's a perfectly normal reaction to difficult or frustrating circumstances. However, it becomes a problem when expressed excessively and it affects your day-to-day activities and interpersonal relationships.

Anger can be anything from mild irritation to rage. It may occasionally be unreasonable or excessive. When it gets to this point, it could be difficult to control your emotions. You could act widely in a way you wouldn't do normally.

Turner (2022) said that although anger is not always associated with ADHD, the two conditions have a significant connection. Stanborough (2021) also said that anger was once included in the definition of ADHD. For instance, ADHD was referred to as a "disorder of anger and aggression" in the United Kingdom. Although anger is no longer one of the criteria used to diagnose ADHD, many medical professionals know it can hinder your ability to function well at home, in school, and your social life.

SO, WHAT'S THE CONNECTION?

ADHD symptoms could make you appear more aggressive. But it might not necessarily be motivated by malicious intent, as is typically the case with proactive, aggressive behavior.

Emotions are frequently felt more strongly by people with ADHD than by those without it. This is also known as emotional dysregulation. If you didn't skip the previous chapter, you would have learned about emotional dysregulation. Some characteristics that accompany this intense emotion are:

- ✓ Outbursts of explosive anger
- ✓ Overreactions to minor stressors
- ✓ Intense emotions
- ✓ Difficulty expressing anger verbally
- ✓ Persistent irritability
- ✓ Increased impatience when stressed

WHAT ARE THE THINGS THAT TRIGGER THESE INTENSE EMOTIONS IN TEENS WITH ADHD?

IMPULSIVITY

Impulsivity is one of the symptoms of ADHD. An inability to concentrate and maintain behavior control is frequently the root cause of impulsivity. Because of their impulsive nature, people with ADHD express their anger immediately. This is more apparent with adolescents.

Saylor and Amann (cited by Low, 2022) stated that impulsive aggression, also known as *affective aggression*, is experienced by more than 50% of preadolescents with ADHD. Impulsive aggression is characterized by strong, unplanned emotions, typically anger, often expressed in the heat of the moment.

 **LOW SELF-ESTEEM**

Low self-esteem is common for people with ADHD, regardless of their age group. Adolescents who suffer from ADHD may have difficulty achieving academic success. In addition, it makes it harder for them to make and keep friends, which can cause them to feel alone and lower their self-esteem.

Anger can also result from this—low self-esteem—and anxiety about a situation they have no control over.

DISRESPECT AND HUMILIATION

Every teenager wants to be treated with respect. In their adolescence, they believe they deserve some level of respect. When they're denied that or humiliated before their peers, family, or in a public space, they go into a rage.

FRUSTRATION

Challenges that get in the way of achieving goals are what cause frustration. Frustration tolerance is the capacity to handle frustration. One of the symptoms of ADHD is a low frustration tolerance. When frustrated, a teenager with ADHD can have an angry outburst.

VIOLATION OF RIGHTS

Just as in the story in my introduction to this chapter, Daniel felt it was his right to have an Xbox. Every time he was denied that right, he exploded. Anytime teens with ADHD are denied what they think they have the right to enjoy, they react intensely with rage.

HYPERACTIVITY

Hyperactivity, or excess energy, can manifest as excessive physical and/or verbal activity. The energy and fretfulness that show up with ADHD might be an excessive amount to bear now and again until it at long last spills over into furious words or actual responses.

UNDERSTANDING THE LEVELS OF EMOTIONAL RAGE

To deal with emotional rage, you need to understand how it builds up and is expressed. In other words, you don't just express emotional rage; there's a process to it. To understand this process is to know how it works and, thus, curb it before it overwhelms you.

Parvez (2022) highlighted stages of emotional rage. Let me walk you through those stages:

THE TRIGGER

There is always a cause of anger, whether internal or external. Life events, negative comments from others, and other things can act as external triggers. Anger can be sparked internally by thoughts and emotions.

When a primary emotion like anxiety is triggered, anger can arise as a secondary emotion as a reaction to your anxiety.

But basically, any information that makes you feel threatened is a trigger for anger. You can still reevaluate the situation at this stage since you're not yet completely engulfed in anger.

THE BUILD UP

A step further from the trigger will bring you to the point where your mind begins to tell you a story about why your anger is justified. This story could be about something that happened recently. This begins to stir fury in you.

At this stage, you can still curb the emotions rising within. You can still shift gears and check to see if the story is true at this point. The rage you're already feeling within will continue to build up if you believe your anger story is legitimate.

GETTING READY TO ACT

Your body begins to prepare you for action once your anger reaches a certain point.

At this point, you'll notice that:

- Your body tightens up to get ready for action.
- Your pupils dilate to get a better look at your foe.
- Your nostrils flare to let in more air.
- Your breathing rate rises to get more oxygen.
- Your heart rate rises to get more oxygen and energy.

Your body is ready to act. At this point, it will be hard to reconsider the situation and let go of your anger. However, with enough mental effort, it is still doable.

THE INTENSE URGE TO ACT

The next step is for your body to push you to take action now that it has prepared you for it. The feeling of this "push" is an urge to act, scream, punch, etc.

THE ACT

It's hard to resist an impulse. The accumulated energy wants to be released quickly.

When you're just mildly irritated, you can fix your anger with little effort if the leak isn't that bad. However, repairing a pipe that leaks like a firehose requires more effort. A firehose that is difficult to close is opened when you act on your anger. You say and do mean things out of hostility in minutes.

Your fight-or-flight survival instinct is in charge at this point. You are unable to reason.

THE RELIEF

Once you explode and release the energy you've accumulated in a short time, how do you feel next? Relieved. It looks like you've just taken off a heavy load. This relief is transient, though.

THE RECOVERY

During the recovery phase, your anger has completely subsided, and you begin to calm down. It's like you've been restored to normalcy, and your senses are back after a temporary moment of madness has passed.

What usually follows afterward are feelings of guilt, shame, regret, or even depression.

I can also tell that at this phase, it looks like we were being possessed by a force higher than us that just used us for its destructive deed and left us to sulk. At least we're able to think straight again.

THE REPAIR

At this final stage, you might want to consider apologizing for your destructive attitude. But it's not always the case with most teens with ADHD. They might feel sober temporarily and try to act differently. Most times, expressing how sorry they are is difficult. They usually feel too ashamed to utter the word.

However, this is the point of repentance, at least until the next trigger comes.

How right is Parvez with his analogy? So, right!

But if this is the case, how do we control it?

HOW TO CONTROL EMOTIONAL RAGE WITH DBT

Do you remember that I spoke extensively about DBT—Dialectical Behavior Therapy—in the first chapter of this book?

Now let's see its application to treating an intense emotion like anger.

When Ciesinski et al. (2022) conducted research on the efficacy of DBT to treat anger and aggressive behavior, they found that DBT significantly reduced anger, though it required longer treatment to get this result. They also discovered that DBT effectively reduced dysregulated anger across different mental disorders.

With this finding, we can go on to apply DBT to treating anger. However, we can't use all the skills you've learned at once. Of the three, let's pick just one.

Which one did you choose? Okay, I'll use emotional regulation here; yay! But if that's not what you picked, it's OK; you can still go on to apply the skill you chose to control emotional rage.

OK, so, let's say you've responded to the trigger, and you're beginning to sense something strong stirring up within you, just before you act on it,

STOP!

Yes! You read that correctly; simply freeze! Let me ask you, who's in charge of you? You or your feelings? Can you see the sign on the road? You're about to rush into another vehicle (or person) at an intersection. If you don't halt immediately, the impact will be disastrous. Do you want that? I doubt it.

So, stop!

Muster all the strength within you to step on the brake pedals immediately. Stop!

Yea, that's right. You just saved yourself from another disastrous event. The last anger you vented that caused a lot of havoc should be your last. Just bring yourself to a halt.

Wondering if it's that easy? Have you tried it? It'll be easier if you do this next thing.

AFFIRMATIVE SELF-TALK

Talk yourself persistently into stopping until you stop. Don't say, "I can't get angry," say, "I don't get angry."

In my observation, if you want this self-talk to be effective, don't think it in your head; say it out loud with your mouth. This is how it works. Your mind is already fired up to act negatively. It's getting ready to throw a hard punch. When you speak loudly with your mouth to counter the signal your mind is about to send into your hand, it freezes it for a moment. When you persist, a counteraction is likely to take place.

So don't just think it; say it. Tell yourself, "No! I don't act brashly." "No! I don't obey my impulses."

Self-talk will also enable you to reframe the situation. You could pause and consider the reasons for your behavior rather than succumbing to anger. Irritation can be turned into curiosity and compassion. That's reframing.

A potent strategy for turning around negative emotions is reframing. Situations have many sides to them. We neutralize an emotional overreaction and instead connect with others by pausing and refocusing instead of acting on our initial emotion.

NOW TAKE A STEP BACK

By now, you should be calm. Now, you can step back from the whole situation and reevaluate what triggered your initial rage.

This can be done mentally or physically by taking a step back. You can use this to free yourself from the strong urge to react.

Take note of your breathing once you've stepped back. You might be breathing slowly or holding your breath. Make an effort to take a few deep, slow breaths.

Give yourself some time to sort through things. Remember that while your feelings may be strong, you are ultimately responsible for your actions.

OBSERVE WHAT'S GOING ON AROUND YOU

Take stock of the things you're going through. What might an outsider say about the situation? Try to notice what's going on without being critical.

Additionally, pay attention to your own mind and body. Are you experiencing muscle tension? Where? Are you weeping profusely on your face? How do they feel when you touch them? Do you clench your jaw? Are you having second thoughts? Which ideas are coming to mind? Is it just one or two of the same? Which is more relevant, the past or the present? Explore your inner and outer experiences with curiosity.

PROCEED MINDFULLY

You've eased some emotion by completing this DBT STOP skill step. Try to think of a wise answer by considering what you would like to happen in the current situation. Which outcome would be in line with your values, wants, and needs? Which outcome will give you the most satisfaction tomorrow or next week? Make an effort to proceed in accordance with these factors.

CHOOSE AN OPPOSITE ACTION

Practicing this technique now is easier because you won't have to apply it when the emotion is still intense.

Now you can easily transform unpleasant emotions into pleasant ones. You can choose a different line of action. The idea behind the opposite action is that taking a positive rather than a negative action can help you deal with negative emotions. By doing this, you avoid doing something harmful and counteract the suffering you might otherwise experience due to the distressing emotion.

In this instance, you're enraged, and there are numerous means by which you could have expressed your anger. But if the action you take is the opposite of how you feel, like walking away from that angry situation or doing something nice to distract yourself, you will have invested your energy in something that will eventually make you feel better. You not only reversed your behavior by walking away rather than yelling at someone, but you also started to change how you felt angry. Instead of escalating or intensifying your feelings, you did something that made them less intense by substituting something positive for them.

It's essential to understand that practicing this skill does not entail controlling your emotions. You are taking a different course of action by making use of your anger. This will cause your feelings to shift over time.

Wow! It's been a tremendous adventure with you up until this point. We've covered two parts of this book already. Can you take stock now? What have you learned so far?

Did you remember what you documented on that plain sheet of paper at the beginning of this adventure? Can you check it again to confirm if you're still on point?

In this chapter, I tried to strip off anger to show you the likely things that cause anger and how anger builds up. There's a point in the build-up of anger where you still have control over it. You'll lose the rein when it exceeds that point. I also showed you how emotional regulation skills can be adopted to control an aggressive emotional outburst. In other words, DBT skills are capable of helping you manage emotional rage. You can respond to things.

What triggers anger in you?

Which DBT skills do you think can work best for you to manage anger?

CHAPTER 7: INTERPERSONAL EFFECTIVENESS SKILLS: A REALISTIC WAY TO IMPROVE YOUR RELATIONSHIPS

> 66 The key to healthy communication is having a willingness to lay aside our defensive tendencies and accept responsibility for our part of the relationship 99

— Asa Don Brown

Are you ready to learn the fourth DBT skill?

Just to clarify, these DBT skills are not independent of one another. You could use two different skills for one issue. This depends on:

1. How well you've practiced and mastered the skills

2. The situation at hand is also a factor.

In the previous chapter, I used only STOP as an example to resolve an anger issue. There could be moments when you'll have to mix it with another skill. The goal isn't to see what skill you used. It's about which one you find most useful for you. The overall goal is your emotional well-being.

Now, about interpersonal effectiveness, let me introduce you to Stet from the 2014 Hollywood preteen movie, *Boychoir*. Stet is one of the lead characters in this movie. He was raised by a single mother who numbs her pain with drugs. And his father hasn't contacted him for 12 years. Stet isn't a privileged young boy. Well, maybe he has every right to be angry at everyone and everything.

Stet is known for his unruly behavior in school. Everywhere he goes, at least one kid irritates him to the point of rage. He doesn't respect teachers. He's always being grounded for one offense or another. This implies that it's hard for Stet to have friends.

Despite his gifted voice and ear for music, Stet will have been a waste, except for his principal, who is ready to overlook his misconduct and give him a chance to harness his gifts.

Dear young reader, relationships are essential to whatever you'll become during your time on Earth. Stet has someone who believes in him. You might think you don't, but there are people who do if you look well. Well, I'm one of those people. And I believe in what you can become. However, when you burn the bridges connecting you with those people, it'll be difficult for them to help you.

Those burned bridges are what the interpersonal effectiveness skill is designed to help you fix and rebuild.

INTRODUCTION TO INTERPERSONAL EFFECTIVENESS SKILLS

Which skill do you consider most valuable?

In the world we live in today, you need to have skills for virtually everything. If you don't have it, you acquire it, or else you'll lose relevance. Our skill set can be expanded, enhanced, and improved in many ways. To improve our lives by developing a specific skill or set of skills, there are thousands of courses, millions of books and articles, and countless tips and suggestions.

But which of those skills is the most significant?

That question may not have a definitive answer, but I believe one of the most common responses would be interpersonal or communication skills.

Do you know how many people you've met in your time on this planet? Countless, I bet. And you'll still meet more people. Without doubt, you'll come into contact with thousands, if not tens of thousands, of people during your lifetime. But you can't impress everyone you meet—that's not possible anyway—and you need to get along with the people around you well enough to survive.

I'm certain about what you just read above. I'm more certain that getting along with other people is a fact that applies to teens with ADHD as well. I know this could be difficult. However, it's not impossible. I'm here to make it possible for you.

WHAT MORE DO YOU NEED TO KNOW ABOUT INTERPERSONAL EFFECTIVENESS SKILLS?

Interpersonal effectiveness is a set of DBT skills that help you establish and maintain healthy relationships with yourself and others. Simply put, it means the capacity to interact with other people.

Mairanz (2019) also added that learning to balance demands and priorities—the things you want and need in your life—is central to the interpersonal effectiveness model in DBT. These skills can be used to navigate relationships with other people and figure out how to get what you need.

Vivyan (2015) suggested four basic things this skill will help you achieve:

✓ It'll empower you to take care of your relationships.

✓ You'll be able to find a balance between what you want and what others want.

✓ You'll be able to find a balance between your "shoulds" and "wants."

✓ You'll develop mastery and respect for yourself.

This is getting more interesting, isn't it?

Overall, the interpersonal effectiveness skills are aimed at three things. This should be your guiding star as you learn and practice these skills. *DBT Self-Help* neatly groups these goals:

✓ Objective Effectiveness – achieve something you want

✓ Relationship Effectiveness – improve or maintain a relationship

✓ Self-Respect Effectiveness – maintain self-respect

A SHORT EXERCISE:

Here's a little exercise I want you to try. Can you try to reflect on your most recent interactions? These are the things you'll consider during your reflection:

✓ How often did I meet all three goals?

✓ Is there any aspect of this framework that I find difficult?

Try to give it some thought and pinpoint the source of the discomfort. Do you have no idea what you want? Do you know how to talk to people in the right way? Are you uncomfortable asking for things?

The purpose of this exercise isn't to judge you. That is not consistent with the ethics of DBT skills. It's not about answering these questions correctly. However, to work toward moving forward, it's essential to investigate the source of our unease.

WHY'S THIS SO IMPORTANT?

You might be curious to know why interpersonal effectiveness warrants this much attention. Well, I've already started talking about the importance of communication earlier. Dr. Linehan (cited by Ackerman, 2017) also believed that these skills were crucial because how we communicate with others significantly impacts the quality of our relationships and the outcomes of those relationships.

In essence, your well-being, self-esteem, confidence, and understanding of who you are become significantly influenced by the quality of your relationships and interactions.

Whew! That is a significant impact that effective communication has on your life.

OK, SO WHAT ARE THE INTERPERSONAL EFFECTIVENESS SKILLS?

These skills are easy to remember with their acronyms:

- THINK
- FAST
- GIVE
- DEAR MAN

THINK

This skill is sort of new in the interpersonal effectiveness skill set. Here's what it means and how it's used:

T – Think

Consider the situation from the other person's point of view. Are they also enraged? Are they judging you as unreasonable in the same way that you judge them?

H – Have empathy

Think about what it's like to be someone else. Give yourself a moment to feel their emotions.

I – Interpretations

Consider the potential causes of their irrational behavior. To get your mind thinking, start with crazy reasons and work your way up to more plausible ones.

N – Notice

Take note of the other party. Pay attention when they try to be nicer and make the relationship better. You might think otherwise but notice how scared they look. You don't have to do anything right now. Just pay attention.

K – Kind

In your response, be kind. This does not necessitate immediate forgiveness and forgetting. You might say, "I hope we can fix this in the future, and what you said hurts." That's kinder than yelling and calling people names.

FAST

FAST assists you in maintaining self-respect during disagreements or discussions. The acronym consists of four skills that teach you how to behave in an argument to achieve your goal at the highest possible level without compromising your own values.

F – be Fair

Be fair to others and yourself. Ensure you're not using dramatic or judgmental thoughts or statements like "I'm powerless in this situation" or "They're the worst!" when you're being fair. Instead, you might wonder, "I didn't agree with most of what he said, but what elements of truth were there?"

A – no Apologies

This doesn't imply that you'll never apologize. Apologizing is really effective in relationships. However, you owe no one an apology if you've done nothing wrong. You shouldn't be sorry for being alive or making a request. You shouldn't apologize for disagreeing or having an opinion, either.

S - Stick to values

Your values are one of your greatest assets, don't sell them out. Don't ever do it for whatever reason. Stick to your guns and be crystal clear about what you consider the moral or valued way of thinking and acting.

T – be Truthful

Never lie. It doesn't suit you. When you are in control, don't act helpless. Do not exaggerate or invent justifications.

THINK AND FAST are two important skills that can help you handle relationship conflicts.

GIVE

GIVE is especially crucial for effective communication to build and keep relationships healthy.

G – be Gentle

Be polite and considerate in your approach. Threats, manipulation, and verbal or physical attacks should be avoided. Avoid all forms of harassment. Avoid making threats with your words. Gentleness demonstrates an awareness of the other person's feelings. The person you're communicating with will be able to feel loved rather than attacked due to this. When no one is defensive, communication is always better.

I – act Interested

Listen to the other person. Pay attention to their viewpoint. Turn to the person, keep eye contact, and instead of leaning away, lean toward them. By maintaining eye contact, actually listening to what is being said, and making a facial expression, you can use body language to show interest.

V – Validate

Show that you comprehend the other person's perspective on the situation. See things from their perspective and say or do what you see. This is like being empathic. You could say, "I know how hard this is for you, and I also see you are busy."

E – Easy manner

Wear a smile. Introduce some light humor. Sweet-talk. Don't bring your attitude with you. Throughout the conversation, project an air of ease and relaxation. You'll be easier to talk to.

DEAR MAN

The DEARMAN skill aims to help us develop healthy relationships with other people and meet our needs through effective interpersonal communication. It's used to effectively and respectfully ask for something that builds and maintains a relationship, regardless of whether you actually get what you ask for.

D – Describe

Describe the situation in a straightforward way. Follow the facts. Describe your exact reaction to the other person.

E – Express

Express your thoughts and feelings regarding the situation. Don't assume the other person understands your feelings.

A – Assert yourself

Clearly and politely ask for what you want or say no to make yourself heard. If you don't ask, don't assume other people will do what you want. Verify that you're assertive without being passive or aggressive.

R – Reinforce

It's more effective to politely tell the other person the importance of what you're requesting and what you might lose if you don't get what you're asking for. This is better than forcing a request. Do you think the other person will gain anything from that, too? Let them know.

M – stay Mindful

Stay focused on your goal, and don't get distracted. Don't be defensive or hostile if the other person starts to do so. Neglect attacks. Ignore the threats, comments, or attempts to divert the conversation if the other person attacks, threatens, or attempts to change the subject. You could practice mindfulness to deal with any overwhelming feelings that may arise.

A – Appear confident

Look competent, confident, and effective. Use your body language and voice to convey confidence. Maintain good eye contact. No muttering, whispering, glancing at the ground or retreating. Don't expect anyone to take your request seriously if you don't take yourself seriously.

N – Negotiate

Recognize that others have limitations of their own. Hence, don't be imposing. Be willing to make some concessions if the need arises. Be reasonable and considerate with your request. You could ask, "What do you think we should do?" or "How can this work?"

You could also make an offer and request additional solutions to the issue. However, be realistic.

10 WAYS TO IMPROVE INTERPERSONAL SKILLS

Consider this a plus in this book. Do you know why? Beyond treating ADHD, this skill will position you for great opportunities in your career. This implies that the earlier you start practicing these skills, the better.

Just like every other soft skill, interpersonal skills can be learned. Sounds great, right?

Here are 10 proven ways you can improve your interpersonal skills:

1. BE A GOOD LISTENER AND A BAD INTERRUPTER

You're accustomed to expressing your opinions, aren't you? The first step in building healthy relationships through this skill is to be a good listener. Give people space and listen to what they have to say. Listening attentively indicates you value what the other person is saying.

It'll also help you understand the message better. Your response will be more precise than when you speak without listening.

Refrain from interrupting people's train of thought or cutting in when they're trying to make their points. Some people are turned off when they're interrupted.

2. BE A GOOD PROCESSOR

As you listen to what the other person is saying and observe the communication trend, patiently process all you hear to give a reasonable and positive response.

3. ACCEPT THE OTHER PERSON

Accept others for who they are because not everyone is like you. You will gain a valuable perspective that will help you deal with them. Don't be judgmental of the other person before or during the conversation. Treat the other person with kindness. It'll create a positive environment for the other person to express their thoughts freely.

4. RESPECT THEIR VIEWS

Respect for oneself is crucial. Respect for other people is crucial in conversations, however. Don't stop at accepting them; respect their views as well. Remember that, even if you disagree with what they're saying, the other person has the right to their own opinion. Wait until they finish speaking before expressing your thoughts on the subject in a non-confrontational manner. Don't pounce on them immediately because they don't share your view. Disagree softly. You could further make them see things from your perspective, but not by yelling.

5. POSITIVE BODY LANGUAGE

Body language is using your voice tone, gestures, gaze, and various postures to convey your intended idea to the person you are communicating with. Ensure your body language doesn't send the wrong signals to the other person.

6. PUT AWAY DISTRACTORS

Do you want to have good communication? Then put away anything that could distract you during the conversation, especially when the other person is talking. You can't tell me you're listening to me when your fingers are dancing on your smartphone's keypad.

Phones are major distractors during conversations today. Teens and young adults are actually fond of this habit. There's always something to check on the phone. But do you know what? Even if you feel compelled to use your phone, resist the urge. Your phone will still be there after the conversation. The other person won't feel valued when you're pressing your phone during a conversation.

7. BE CLEAR

You can't just give your listeners only half-baked information and leave them hanging. Always ensure that you provide all the available information, even if there are still details to follow. It goes without saying that using words that are easy to understand is important to avoid confusion.

8. BE STRAIGHTFORWARD

Be direct and straightforward whenever there is a concern or issue so that people will understand what you want and what needs to be done. It will be difficult for others to take you seriously if you avoid the conversation or postpone making your point.

9. CHOOSE A GOOD PACE

You don't have to speak too quickly or too slowly to get your point across effectively. Know when to deliberately slow down, when to pause for emphasis, and when to speed up. The listening experience of your audience can be impacted by speed. You need to ensure that you are speaking at the appropriate pace if you want your listener to comprehend your message effectively.

10. MAINTAIN EYE CONTACT

Although it can be challenging, truly looking someone in the eye is a necessary part of having meaningful conversations. The person you speak with feels validated and understood when you maintain eye contact.

This nonverbal cue also informs the other person that you're paying attention to what they're saying. Don't even try looking at the floor or outside the window. It indicates you're not interested in what the other person is saying.

SEVEN SELF-EVALUATION PHRASES FOR INTERPERSONAL EFFECTIVENESS SKILLS

Let's take a quick assessment of your current level of interpersonal skills now that you've learned how to improve them. The result will let you know which areas to focus on while improving this skill.

I'll list seven areas here. Rate yourself on a scale of 1 to 10.

✓ Shows the ability to actively listen to other people's conversations without interrupting them.

✓ Communicates clearly and concisely, making it simple for others to comprehend what is being communicated.

✓ Disagrees with grace and respect when the other person doesn't share my view.

✓ Communicate with a positive attitude always.

✓ Assertive and demonstrates self-respect and comprehensible communication

✓ Have an awkward sense of humor and am always pissing others off.

✓ Difficult to approach me or begin a conversation with me.

What's your current state?

There's always room for improvement. Don't stop practicing.

GAMES & ACTIVITIES FOR GROUPS TO DEVELOP EFFECTIVE INTERPERSONAL SKILLS

Let's try to introduce some fun activities to spice up these practices. You can play these games to develop and improve your interpersonal skills. Of course, you can't play these games alone. You need a partner or more. Your partner or co-player could be from your family, a peer, or a neighbor.

Try this,

 1. **CAN YOU HEAR ME NOW?**

"Can you hear me now?" is one of the simplest games involving virtual communication. Participants need paper and pens to play the game. Each round, one player describes an object for the other players to draw one line or shape at a time, for instance, a cat, a stoplight, the sun, or a tree. The game requires the players to attempt to guess the object before the drawing is finished.

The game demonstrates how simple statements can have unexpected interpretations and stresses the significance of clear instructions. Additionally, it's entertaining to observe the finished drawings.

 2. **YES?**

"Yes?" is one of the communication games with the most energy. The activity's most crucial form of communication is eye contact. Form a circle. Then the participant whose turn it is looks across the circle at a teammate and inquires, "Yes?" which the teammate states is "Yes." The players then switch positions. Players can create new chains as the game progresses, allowing multiple players to speak or move simultaneously. The more active the chains, the more difficult it is for players to focus and respond. In a busy environment, this game teaches players to remain alert and multitask.

BLINDFOLD STROLL

To play this game, here is what you need to do:

✓ Set up an obstacle course with one player blindfolded.

✓ Have other players shout instructions to the blindfolded player as they move through the course.

You can time course completion or introduce penalties and traps to make the game more fun and exciting. Regardless of how you play it, this activity emphasizes the importance of giving precise instructions and gives teammates a chance to practice giving each other directions.

ANOTHER WAY TO SAY

The game, Another Way to Say, requires players to come up with alternative phrases and synonyms. The round begins with a single player saying a phrase. The other players come up with similar sayings until they run out of options.

The exercise can be a last-man-standing competition in which the player with the most contributions wins the round, or it can be a collaborative effort to generate phrases. The game's goal is to demonstrate how many different ways a thought can be expressed.

Players are encouraged to try to develop new phrases and use descriptive language, but the group can also challenge creative responses.

There are many other games you can play to practice your interpersonal skills. You can look them up on the internet.

SOME WAYS TO IMPROVE YOUR INTERPERSONAL EFFECTIVENESS AT SCHOOL AND HOME

This aspect of learning isn't restricted to teens with ADHD alone. I recommend that teachers and parents encourage these skills in their teens. Hence, while your teenage child or student is learning this, be around to encourage them.

GOOD COMMUNICATION BEGINS AT HOME

Most teens spend most of their early years of development at home with their family. Hence, any habit or culture they grow up with starts at home.

As ADHD teens learn to improve their communication skills, they need to practice with those they spend time with the most—family. Therefore, parents must encourage their teens to build confidence and support healthy communication.

PRACTICE FRIENDLINESS

Being friendly to other people is another way to improve your ability to interact with other people. Smiling and saying "hi" to everyone you see is all it takes to accomplish this. Parents and teachers should learn how to engage teens who struggle with ADHD. Basically, they should ask them how they spent their day.

Learn to engage in eye contact with everyone you meet throughout the day. Always smile. Don't fake the smile. It could seem weird and maybe difficult but keep practicing.

BUILD POSITIVE SELF-TALKS

Instead of telling yourself that no one wants to talk to you because you used to yell at people, try to replace it with positive self-talk. No one will know you've started working on becoming a better communicator until you try engaging people.

Push yourself to step out through a series of positive self-talks:

- ✓ I'm a good listener
- ✓ I don't yell at people
- ✓ I'm calm
- ✓ I'm a good friend
- ✓ I'm at ease around others
- ✓ I'm a team player

You could try this and many more to get yourself going and never relent.

This chapter introduced you to another crucial DBT skill. And like every other skill you've learned so far in this book, interpersonal skills require lots of practice. You must be consistent to get the required result. This chapter emphasized the importance of communication in having good relationships. If you're poor at communicating, you'll lose many friends and have no one to help you when you need them.

This chapter also offered hope for restoring and rebuilding bridges in relationships through practicable skills.

Just before you think you can't do it, step out first. I believe you can do this. Don't relent after a few difficult attempts. Push past that level. You're doing just fine.

> Which relationship will you like to restore?

> What will you do differently now that you know about this skill?

CHAPTER 8: THE PATH TO POSITIVE EMOTIONS AND IMPROVING YOUR MOOD

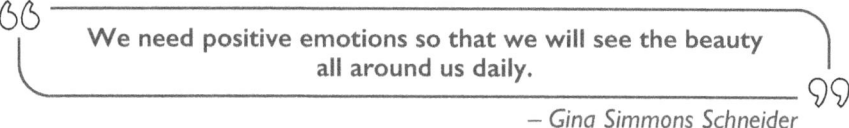

> We need positive emotions so that we will see the beauty all around us daily.

— *Gina Simmons Schneider*

Hannah had been anxious all her life; at 13, it became too much to contain. She was certain that her friends no longer liked her, and she was terrified of failing in school. She constantly fought with her mother and lashed out at her friends. She would scream and cry at the smallest things. Out of concern, Jill, her mother, finally took steps to help Hannah.

Finally, Hannah learned how to control her emotions and develop a sense of self-assurance and positivity due to her participation in dialectical behavioral therapy. She asserted that she was a hundred percent happier. She became a better student, friend, daughter, sister—everything.

In this book's final part, I'll show you the power that lies in building positive emotions. In the opening part of this chapter, Hannah turns out to be a better human by exuding positive emotions.

Just so you know, emotions let out a powerful, invisible scent. It could alter the state of an environment. It's difficult for anyone to laugh where people gather to mourn. It's difficult for anyone to make a joke when someone is letting out intense rage.

As our journey together in this book winds down, I want to give you something like a prelude to my final words.

Dear young friend, emotions are powerful—positive or negative—and could alter your destiny. According to psychologist and expert on emotional wellness at the University of North Carolina, Chapel Hill, Dr. Barbara L. Fredrickson (cited by the NIH, 2015), having a positive outlook doesn't mean you'll never experience negative emotions like sadness or anger.

In the right circumstances, any emotion, positive or negative, can change. It would appear that striking a balance between the two is the key. Fredrickson explains that while positive emotions expand our awareness and expose us to novel concepts, allowing us to develop and enhance our survival arsenal, negative emotions are necessary for people to cope with difficult circumstances and act appropriately in the short term. However, negative emotions that are unrelated to what is actually taking place in the moment and are based on excessive pondering about the past or worrying about the future can lead to problems.

Wouldn't it be wise to settle for positive emotions? To create a life worth living, increasing positive emotions is essential.

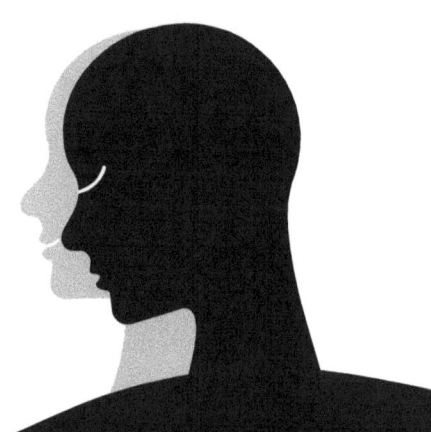

THE POWER OF POSITIVE EMOTIONS

Have you ever been told that all you have to do to make things work out is "stay positive"? Having optimism is a wonderful quality, but it takes more than just hoping for the best to cultivate it. Like I've been emphasizing from the beginning of this adventure, it will require an ongoing routine of practices to cultivate positive emotions throughout your life.

You wouldn't hit the gym for a few days to quit when you've not built enough muscle, would you?

Positive feelings are more than just "a nice feeling." Positive emotions have been shown by science to have a hidden value that directly affects (and improves) your day-to-day well-being.

In an interview with *BeWell*, Barbara Fredrickson said that positive emotions are like nutrients. In more ways than ever, science is demonstrating that, despite the fact that moments of happiness, gratitude, or serenity may appear fleeting and insignificant, they have a significant impact on the way our brains function. According to Fredrickson, such fleeting moments can have the following effects on us:

✓ Allow our mindsets to become more expansive and adaptable.

✓ Our resilience and resourcefulness become heightened.

That's what Fredrickson said gave birth to the broaden-and-build theory of positive emotions.

Isn't it amazing how small moments of joy add up to help us become better versions of ourselves?

TeensHealth specifically noted that positive emotions influence our brains in ways that improve our awareness, attention, and memory. They assist us in taking in more information, remembering multiple concepts at once, and comprehending how concepts relate to one another.

We can learn and improve our skills better when we experience positive emotions that open our minds to new possibilities. As a result, you'll do better on tests and tasks.

Positive emotions make you happier, healthier, and more able to learn and get along with others. That's just how Hannah felt.

DBT ENHANCES POSITIVE EMOTIONS

The essence of this book is to emphasize how you can build positive emotions using DBT skills. Hannah in our opening story and other examples in previous chapters, especially those with ADHD, could translate negativity into positivity using DBT. Don't forget this.

You could achieve positive emotions through different means; however, DBT skills are one of the few proven ways you could apply and practice to achieve such a level of positivity.

I must remind you why DBT is effective in this regard:

✓ DBT teaches you how to deal with negative feelings and encourages you to keep positive ones in your collection. That's part of what you learned on emotional regulation skills, right?

✓ It teaches you how to control your emotions instead of letting them control you.

✓ DBT makes you less likely to experience negative emotions and helps you to build more positive emotional experiences.

✓ DBT teaches that having a bank of positive emotions can assist you in preventing the outburst or persistence of negative emotions.

✓ Most importantly, DBT doesn't deny the existence of negative emotions. Increasing your positive emotions doesn't negate your negative feelings. It's a way to broaden your horizons and offer other options during trying times.

STILL STRUGGLING WITH SYMPTOMS OF ADHD AS A TEEN?

Let me emphasize to you again. You might have had it rough and difficult trying to cope with those outbursts of anger. You might struggle to build healthy relationships with others, especially your family, but don't quit trying.

A neurodevelopmental disorder like ADHD can be corrected through the consistent practice of behavioral reordering skills like DBT.

To quit trying is to allow negativism to overwhelm you. It's a positive attitude that will make you keep on practicing the skills you've been exposed to in this book.

WHAT ARE POSITIVE AND NEGATIVE EMOTIONS?

Fredrickson already stated the place of positive and negative emotions and their presence in some situations we face.

Let's say you begin making a list of all the feelings you've ever felt. Try it right now, just for fun.

What did you come up with? I bet such expressions like happy, sad, excited, ashamed, angry, depressed, fearful, grateful, proud, scared, confused, stressed, relaxed, etc., would come up naturally.

You will notice that these emotions are not one-sided. A careful observation will reveal that there are emotions that are positive and others that are negative.

Now, being human necessitates the ability to experience both positive and negative emotions. Although we may use the term "negative" to describe more difficult feelings, this doesn't imply that they are undesirable or that we shouldn't experience them.

However, most people would probably rather experience a positive emotion than a negative one. You'd probably prefer to be happy rather than sad or confident rather than insecure.

TeensHealth said that the amount of each type of emotion, whether positive or negative, that we experience is what matters. This is how our emotions are balanced.

DOES THAT MEAN WE NEED BOTH?

If you took a look at every negative emotion you've ever felt, do you ever wish to experience any of those feelings? You probably don't—just what I thought—because no one ever wishes for such feelings. There's literally nothing good about having any of those negative feelings.

How about the positive emotions? Of course! Everyone wants always to have a pleasant and loving feeling. No one ever thinks to themselves and says, "Oh, I wish I wasn't experiencing this emotion."

You don't need negative emotions to thrive, grow, and/or be effective in different contexts of function. But Fredrickson said negative feelings—at least moderately—also have their place.

What! What would you do with negative emotions?

NEGATIVE EMOTIONS?

Yeah, Ackerman (2019) stated that positive psychology isn't all about positive emotions alone. According to Ackerman, we must experience negative emotions to live a full and rewarding life. They're an inevitable part of life.

Perhaps if you pay a little more attention to the effects of negative feelings, you'll realize their purpose. For instance, usually, preparation is compelled by stress. You can protect yourself by being angry. You can accept an apology and make amends with guilt. Those are subtle ways negative emotions could serve a good purpose.

There are other ways negative emotions could be purposeful in your life:

- ✅ They alert us to potential dangers or difficulties that we need to face. Fear, for instance, can make us aware of potential danger. It suggests that we might need to safeguard ourselves.

- ✅ We can tell when someone is behaving inappropriately, crossing a line, or betraying our trust by feeling angry. Anger can indicate that we may need to take action on our own.

✓ They assist us in narrowing down an issue so we can address it.

✓ Anxiety could help us to prepare and plan for what's to come.

✓ Disgust could make us reject what we feel isn't healthy for us.

However, just like Fredrickson stated, experiencing excessive negative emotions can lead to feelings of overwhelm, anxiety, exhaustion, and stress. Problems might appear to be too big to handle when negative emotions are out of balance.

The more we dwell on negative emotions, the more negative we become. Concentrating on the negative only makes it worse.

HOW ABOUT POSITIVE EMOTIONS?

I've shared some basic things about positive emotions with you in the previous session and some previous chapters. However, you need to know that the field of positive psychology believes that learning how to adapt to negative emotions and effectively deal with them is just as important as learning how to boost our positive emotions and take advantage of the opportunities they present.

Ackerman (2019) also stated that we give ourselves the best chance of living a balanced and meaningful life when we can accept, embrace, and take advantage of both our positive and negative emotions. Because of this, the discipline of positive psychology is wary of emphasizing positive feelings too much; it's just as essential to comprehend how to transform negative feelings into positive experiences as it is to take advantage of our positive feelings.

So, the question again is, "Do you need both?" Yes! However, don't dwell excessively on the negatives. It could be harmful.

Here's how I believe you can balance the two emotions:

✓ Build your positive emotions to outweigh the negative ones.

✓ Every day, try to be positive.

Did you grasp that?

BENEFITS OF POSITIVE EMOTIONS

The "broaden-and-build" theory of positive emotions helps you understand how having positive emotions is essential for thriving in daily life and fostering mental wellness. Emotions of positivity assist you in expanding your experience and perspective. They can also develop crucial relationships and skills essential to maximizing performance.

Further studies show that positive emotions shape our lives. Rather than being limited to a single aspect of life, these effects pervade every nook and cranny of the human experience. They help with personal growth and fulfillment as well as improve relationships in the workplace, classrooms, and with families.

Gordon (n.d.) stated that a positive attitude is more than just a nice way to live. It's the right way to live.

Here are other benefits of positive emotions:

GREATER RESILIENCE

A study found that emotional regulation, which helps people recover from stressful situations and find meaning in them, was significantly impacted by increased resilience. Higher rates of empathy, cooperation, assertiveness, and self-control were found in students who participated in a program aimed at boosting resilience in schoolchildren.

Positive emotions can also help people learn how to deal with difficult situations.

Overall, you can remain more resilient in the face of challenges if you find ways to experience a little positive emotion each day. To effectively deal with adversity, it's helpful to consume a healthy diet rich in positive emotions to reduce stress.

IMPROVED OUTCOMES RELATED TO PERFORMANCE

You can become more creative when you feel positive emotions. Positive emotions can encourage you to think more creatively about solving a problem if you've been stuck trying to solve it for a long time. Positive emotions also make you more receptive to new concepts, challenges, and opportunities. Throughout the process of learning something new or mastering a new skill, you frequently experience these feelings.

Positive emotions can lead to improvements in academics, physical and mental health, social relationships, community involvement, and more. That's what gives you a life worth living.

MAKE NEW CONNECTIONS

Have you ever entered a room where everyone was having a good time laughing, and you couldn't help but join in, even though you didn't know what the other people were laughing about? Positive feelings spread like wildfire. They promote social interaction. Positive emotions not only make you more receptive to other people, but they also help other people become more receptive to you.

AID IN YOUR RELAXATION AND RESET

Do you remember the last time you were really angry? What happened? Did you remember that your heart rate accelerated, you felt agitated, or maybe you sweated? The benefit of positive emotion in that context is that, after experiencing the physical effects of negative emotions, positive emotions can assist you in quicker body recovery. Emotional well-being is essential for reviving and maintaining energy.

In addition, you must know that positive emotions don't grow out of the blues. For instance, in the academic context, positive emotions are facilitated by levels of self-motivation and contentment with learning materials. According to some studies, this indicates positive emotions facilitate learning and contribute to academic achievement.

NEGATIVITY BIAS

Now, if I ask you, "Would you always like to have positive emotions?" I know you won't say no. But I've found out that, although many people, especially teens with neurodevelopmental disorders, wish to always express positive emotions, they find it difficult to do so. The question then is, "Why?"

Why is it difficult to build or express positive emotions regularly?

It's because of something called "negative bias."

OK. SO WHAT DOES THAT MEAN?

Frothingham (2019) stated that negative bias tends to work this way, focusing on negative experiences and considering them to be more important to us—humans—than positive or neutral experiences. Even when those negative experiences are insignificant or unimportant, we frequently focus on them.

Consider the following scenario: you are on vacation with your family and have decided to stay in a nice hotel. Then, at night, you saw a large spider in the sink when you entered the bathroom. Which do you believe will be remembered more clearly: the room's beautiful decor and fine furnishings or the spider you encountered?

The spider experience will linger longer.

According to *Human Performance Resources,* you can successfully navigate a dangerous world because the human brain has evolved to recognize threats and obstacles. Warfighters, their families, and teammates all benefit from this ability by keeping an eye out for danger. However, it can also lead to a negative outlook on life.

We don't know how or when this happened, but it appears that our brain is programmed to prioritize, seek out, and latch onto negative information. This hardwired tendency is what is known as "negativity bias." Negative experiences are more likely to be absorbed by your brain than positive ones.

SHOULDN'T WE JUST QUIT TRYING TO BUILD POSITIVITY SINCE WE'VE BEEN WIRED TO LATCH ONTO NEGATIVES?

No! I don't think so.

Our brains can be reprogrammed to embrace positivity. We can overwrite that negative coding in our brains.

HOW CAN WE OVERRIDE A "DEFAULT" BIAS PROGRAM IN THE BRAIN?

✓ Focus on valuing and appreciating the positive aspects of your life.

✓ Practice mindfulness. Be mindful of what is and isn't important to you.

✓ Break the pattern of negative reactions.

✓ Allow positive experiences to deeply register in your consciousness.

- ✓ Create a portfolio of positive emotions.

- ✓ Engage in uplifting conversation with others.

Before you quit trying, practice these few tips to overwrite the default negative coding in your brain.

New habits, reactions, and emotions can be formed. Nothing can stand between you and your resolve to be a better young adult gunning for a life worth living.

In this final chapter, you've learned the positive and negative sides of emotions. Both are important; you simply need to have fewer negative emotions. You need more positive emotions. And this comes with lots of benefits, as you've learned here.

> What positive emotions will you like to cultivate?

> How often do you need to practice cultivating that emotion?

> If faced with challenges while cultivating this positive emotion, what will you do?

FINAL NOTE

I'm glad you stuck through to the end of this adventure. But this is how far we can go together, for now.

This is just the end of a phase of this journey. It's the beginning of a new phase of adventure for you, dear reader. You've learned so much and experienced a lot of mind shifts in the course of this adventure; now it's time to experience much more.

It's time for applications. It's time to practice those new models I shared with you in this book, acquire new skills in DBT, and go on to live a happy and fulfilling life.

Let me remind you of a few important points.

- ✓ DBT isn't just for adults; preteens and adolescents, including you, can benefit greatly from it as well.

- ✓ DBT isn't a quick-fix scheme. It's a therapeutic program that could serve as a life tool. You could take it anywhere because emotions can be expressed anywhere, at any time.

- ✓ You begin to experience transformation when you accept your reality. Don't deny the fact that you have a behavioral disorder that has cost you a lot. In DBT, change only begins to occur after acceptance.

- ✓ ADHD is a disorder that can be corrected. It's not a hopeless situation. Don't conclude on your situation based on the intensity of your negative emotions. DBT skills offer you a way out.

- ✓ You can choose to re-order this behavioral disorder through DBT skills.

- ✓ Mindfulness is a DBT skill that helps to free your mind of the anxiety of the past and fear of the future to begin to live in the moment.

- ✓ Detailed appreciation for life and everything that makes your life worth living is a crucial practice that makes you mindful of the present moment.

- ✓ You're unique. Your situation is peculiar to you. There's a unique DBT skill for you. Find it and start practicing it. You're not meant to practice all the skills. Discover the one that suits you and your situation. Then start applying and practicing it.

- ✓ The best way to get the best from all you've learned in this book is through consistent practice. Don't quit when the results aren't trickling in. Channel your energy into some more practice. While you're at it, you begin to notice your changes in bits.

I'd like to give you this final piece as a gift to light up your path for the next phase of your journey.

The greatest and most positive emotion you can ever express is love. This isn't just that mushy feeling you have for your lover. Although love is many things to different people, it has different definitions and is expressed by different people in different ways.

However, one paramount thing about *love* is that it makes you consider others before you carry out any action or react in certain ways. You'll be careful to act rashly against anyone you love because you won't want to hurt them. Love also makes you a force of light that people will gravitate toward. Love conquers negativism and compels you to commit yourself to becoming a better version of yourself.

In my view, love is the foundation of all positive emotions. Cultivate a life of love, and you're headed towards a peaceful and happy life.

Keep living right. I'm rooting for you!

If this book has helped you or someone you recommended it to, I look forward to hearing from you. Leave a note for me on Amazon.

Cheers!

GET THIS EXCLUSIVE

5-minute Audio Guided Meditation

To help safely **MANAGE YOUR TEEN'S** sudden emotional meltdown.

and more mindfulness resources...

JOURNALS & SELF-CARE PLANERS

COLORING BOOKS

SCAN QR CODE TO GET YOUR COPY

MESSAGE FROM THE AUTHOR

I truly hope you found this book enjoyable and gained valuable insights from its contents.

If you could spare a moment to share your honest feedback or leave a star-rating on Amazon, I would greatly appreciate it.

(Rating only takes a few clicks).

Your review can guide other young adults to explore this book and potentially aid them on their personal journeys. Plus, it might just bring some good karma your way.

SCAN QR CODE TO
GET YOUR COPY

REFERENCES

5 Tips to Improve Your Self-Talk. (n.d.).

> 5 Tips to Improve Your Self-Talk. Retrieved February 2, 2023, from
> https://psychcentral.com/blog/5-tips-to-improve-your-self-talk

A. (2019, July 22).

> *14 Signs of ADHD: Does Your Child Have ADHD? - ADHD Ireland.* ADHD Ireland.
> Retrieved January 27, 2023, from
> https://adhdireland.ie/14-signs-of-adhd-does-your-child-have-adhd/

Ackerman, C. E. (2017, December 29).

> *Interpersonal Effectiveness: 9 Worksheets & Examples (+ PDF).*
> PositivePsychology.com. Retrieved February 7, 2023, from
> https://positivepsychology.com/interpersonal-effectiveness/

Ackerman, C. E. (2019, April 27).

> *What are Positive and Negative Emotions and Do We Need Both?*
> PositivePsychology.com. Retrieved February 7, 2023, from
> https://positivepsychology.com/positive-negative-emotions/

Badcock, P.B., Friston, K.J., & Ramstead, M.J.D. (2019).

> The hierarchically mechanistic mind: A free-energy formulation of the human
> psyche. Physics of Life Reviews. DOI: 10.1016/j.plrev.2018.10.002

Brillante, D. J. (2020, November 18).

> *Dialectical Behavior Therapy (DBT) for Teens Part I: What It Is and What it Helps With -*
> Expert CBT, DBT, and Testing for Children, Adolescents, and Families.
> Retrieved January 27, 2023, from
> https://centerforcbt.org/2020/11/18/dbt-for-teens-part-1/

Cheung, J. C., Chen, E. Y., McCloskey, M. S., (2022, July 1).

> *The effect of dialectical behavior therapy on anger and aggressive behavior: A systematic*
> *review with meta-analysis - PubMed.* PubMed. Retrieved February 2, 2023, from
> https://pubmed.ncbi.nlm.nih.gov/35609374/

Ciesinski, N. K., Sorgi-Wilson, K. M., *Emotion Regulation in Teens with ADHD*
- CHADD. (n.d.).

> CHADD. Retrieved February 2, 2023, from

https://chadd.org/adhd-news/adhd-news-caregivers/emotion-regulation-in-teens-with-adhd/

Compitus, D. K. (2020, October 1).

What Are Distress Tolerance Skills? The Ultimate DBT Toolkit. PositivePsychology.com. Retrieved February 2, 2023, from https://positivepsychology.com/distress-tolerance-skills/

Cuncic, A. (2022, November 14).

What Is Dysregulation? Verywell Mind. Retrieved February 2, 2023, from https://www.verywellmind.com/what-is-dysregulation-5073868

DBT for Attention Deficit Hyperactivity Disorder (ADHD); DBT Center of Marin. (n.d.).

DBT Center of Marin. Retrieved January 27, 2023, from https://dbtmarin.com/dbt-for-attention-deficit-hyperactivity-disorder

DBT Skills Group: Rules and Resources - Psychotherapy Academy. (n.d.).

Psychotherapy Academy. Retrieved January 27, 2023, from https://psychotherapyacademy.org/dbt/starting-a-dbt-skills-group/

DBT: What Is Dialectical Behavior Therapy? - Child Mind Institute. (n.d.).

Child Mind Institute. Retrieved January 27, 2023, from https://childmind.org/article/dbt-dialectical-behavior-therapy/

Dialectical Behavior Therapy: Children and Preadolescents - Child Mind Institute. (n.d.).

Child Mind Institute. Retrieved January 27, 2023, from https://childmind.org/care/areas-of-expertise/mood-disorders-center/dialectical-behavior-therapy-children-and-preadolescents/

Frothingham, S. (2019, December 16).

Do you have a negativity bias? What Is Negativity Bias? Retrieved February 7, 2023, from https://www.healthline.com/health/negativity-bias

Fung, T. T., Long, M. W., Hung, P., & Cheung, L. W. (2016, July).

An Expanded Model for Mindful Eating for Health Promotion and Sustainability: Issues and Challenges for Dietetics Practice. Journal of the Academy of Nutrition and Dietetics, 116(7), 1081–1086. https://doi.org/10.1016/j.jand.2016.03.013

Gordon. (n.d.).

> *11 BENEFITS OF BEING POSITIVE.* Retrieved February 7, 2023, from
> https://jongordon.com/positive-tip-11-benefits.html#:~:text=The%20research%20
> is%20clear.,It's%20the%20way%20to%20live

Greene, D. P. (2020, July 27).

> *DBT: IMPROVE the Moment – How to Make Crises Bearable.* Manhattan Center for
> Cognitive Behavioral Therapy. Retrieved February 2, 2023, from
> https://www.manhattancbt.com/archives/1699/dbt-improve-the-moment/

Greene, D. P. (2020, August 3).

> *The DBT STOP Skill: How to Not Make a Bad Situation Worse.* Manhattan Center for
> Cognitive Behavioral Therapy. Retrieved February 2, 2023, from
> https://www.manhattancbt.com/archives/1723/dbt-stop-skill/

Halmøy, A., Ring, A. E., Gjestad, R., Møller, M., Ubostad, B., Lien, T.,
Munkhaugen, E. K., & Fredriksen, M. (2022, November 28).

> *Dialectical behavioral therapy-based group treatment versus treatment as usual for
> adults with attention-deficit hyperactivity disorder: a multicenter randomized controlled
> trial - BMC Psychiatry.* BioMed Central. Retrieved January 27, 2023, from
> https://bmcpsychiatry.biomedcentral.com/articles/10.1186/s12888-022-04356-6

Hanh TN, Cheung L. Savor (2010)

> *Mindful Eating, Mindful Life.* HarperCollins Publishers.

History of DBT: Origins and Foundations - Psychotherapy Academy. (n.d.).

> Psychotherapy Academy. Retrieved January 27, 2023, from
> https://psychotherapyacademy.org/dbt/history-of-dialectical-behavioral-therapy-a-
> very-brief-introduction/

> *How DBT Helped Me Cope With BPD | Real Stories.* (n.d.).

> YoungMinds. Retrieved January 27, 2023, from
> https://www.youngminds.org.uk/young-person/blog/how-dbt-gave-me-freedom-fr
> om-borderline-personality-disorder/

> *Interpersonal Effectiveness* - DBT Self Help. (n.d.).

> DBT Self Help. Retrieved February 7, 2023, from
> https://dbtselfhelp.com/dbt-skills-list/interpersonal-effectiveness/

> Linehan, M. (n.d.).

> *Emotional Regulation Skills - Dialectical Behavior Therapy (DBT) Tools.* Dialectical
> Behavior Therapy (DBT) Tools. Retrieved February 2, 2023, from
> https://dbt.tools/emotional_regulation/index.php

Littman, E. (2022, July 11).

How Dysregulated Emotions Hijack the Teen ADHD Brain. ADDitude. Retrieved February 2, 2023, from https://www.additudemag.com/dysregulated-adhd-teens-relationships-social-media-support/

Low, K. (2022, December 22).

ADHD and Anger: How Are They Connected? Verywell Mind. Retrieved February 2, 2023, from https://www.verywellmind.com/understanding-adhd-children-and-anger-20540

Mairanz, A. (2019, December 6).

Interpersonal Effectiveness: Practicing a DBT Skill. DBT Therapist NYC. Empower Your Mind Therapy. Retrieved February 7, 2023, from https://eymtherapy.com/blog/practice-interpersonal-effectiveness-dbt-skill/

Ohwovoriole, T. (2021, May 28).

How to Manage Your Anger. Verywell Mind. Retrieved February 2, 2023, from https://www.verywellmind.com/what-is-anger-5120208

Partington, D. P. (2021, March 19).

Dbt Stories: Mindfulness Practice – Dialectical Behavior Therapy. Retrieved January 27, 2023, from https://dbtforlife.com/2021/03/19/dbt-stories-mindfulness-practice/

Parvez, H. (2022, February 9).

8 Stages of anger in psychology - PsychMechanics. PsychMechanics. Retrieved February 2, 2023, from https://www.psychmechanics.com/stages-of-anger/

Pierper, J. (2020, June 23).

DBT for Teens: How It Works, Examples, & Effectiveness. Retrieved from https://www.choosingtherapy.com/dbt-for-teens/

Positive Emotions and Your Health. (2017, May 4).

NIH News in Health. Retrieved February 7, 2023, from https://newsinhealth.nih.gov/2015/08/positive-emotions-your-health

Rigby, A. (n.d.).

12 Emotional Regulation Skills to Calm Inner Chaos. Retrieved February 2, 2023, from https://www.fingerprintforsuccess.com/blog/emotional-regulation-skills

S. (2021, July 28).

A Beginner's Guide to Distress Tolerance. Sokya Health. Retrieved February 2, 2023, from https://sokyahealthdev.wpengine.com/connection/tipp-a-beginners-guide-to-distress-tolerance/

Saline, S. (2020, February 14).

Q: My Teenage Son's Anger Is Frightening Me — Help! ADDitude. Retrieved

February 2, 2023, from
https://www.additudemag.com/dealing-with-anger-teen-adhd/

Schwartz, B. (2022, September 15).

Self-Soothing: What it is, Benefits, & Techniques to Get Started. Choose Therapy
https://www.choosingtherapy.com/self-soothing/

Stanborough, R. J. (2021, March 30).

ADHD and Anger: How They Are Connected. ADHD and Anger: How They Are
Connected. Retrieved February 2, 2023, from
https://www.healthline.com/health/adhd/adhd-and-anger

*The importance of positive emotions for performance optimization, mental health, and
strong relationships.* (2021, September 27).

HPRC. Retrieved February 7, 2023, from
https://www.hprc-online.org/social-fitness/relationship-building/importance-positi
ve-emotions-performance-optimization-mental

Turner, M. (2022, October 19).

ADHD & Anger: Connection & Treatments. Choosing Therapy.
https://www.choosingtherapy.com/adhd-anger/

Understanding Your Emotions (for Teens) - Nemours KidsHealth. (n.d.).

Understanding Your Emotions (for Teens) - Nemours KidsHealth. Retrieved
February 2, 2023, from https://kidshealth.org/en/teens/understand-emotions.html

Vivyan, C. (2015).

Interpersonal Effectiveness. Get.gg - Getselfhelp.co.uk. Retrieved February 7, 2023,
from https://www.getselfhelp.co.uk/interpersonal-effectiveness/

W. (2016, April 1).

The power of positive emotions - Stanford BeWell. Stanford BeWell. Retrieved
February 7, 2023, from
https://bewell.stanford.edu/the-power-of-positive-emotions/

Wexelblatt, R. (2020, December 29).

Q: My ADHD Teen Reacts Aggressively to Limits! ADDitude. Retrieved February 2,
2023, from
https://www.additudemag.com/anger-issues-teens-adhd-contain-behavior/

Smith, A. (2022, October 31).

DBT Success Stories; My Dialectical Life. DBT Success Stories; My Dialectical Life.
Retrieved January 27, 2023, from
https://www.mydialecticallife.com/dbt-success-stories

OTHER SOURCES

https://childmind.org/article/how-hannah-got-happy/

https://www.goodreads.com/quotes/tag/interpersonal-skills

https://www.goodreads.com/quotes/tag/positive-emotions

https://www.theminiadhdcoach.com/blog/adhd-teenager

https://www.chop.edu/stories/adhd-and-emotional-control-theos-story

https://www.goodreads.com/quotes/tag/distress

https://www.goodreads.com/quotes/tag/emotional-regulation

https://www.goodreads.com/quotes/tag/anger

https://newroadstreatment.org/annies-story-a-healing-journey-with-dbt/

https://www.therecoveryvillage.com/mental-health/stress/stress-statistics/#:~:text=America n%20Institute%20of%20Stress%20Statistics&text=About%2033%20percent%20of%20people ,trouble%20sleeping%20because%20of%20stress

https://www.singlecare.com/blog/news/stress-statistics/

https://www.hopetherapyandwellness.com/blog/157559-what-is-mindfulness-and-how-does-it-help-with-dbt

https://positivepsychology.com/mindfulness-quotes/

https://www.goodreads.com/quotes/tag/dbt#:~:text=Dialectical%20behavior%20therapy%20 depends%20on,%2C%20not%20acceptance%20or%20change.%E2%80%9D&text=%E2%80% 9CKeeping%20a%20stiff%20upper%20lip,does%20hurt%20to%20be%20invalidated.%E2%80 %9D

https://www.hopeforbpd.com/borderline-personality-disorder-treatment/quotes-about-dbt

https://researchoutreach.org/articles/explaining-mind-works-new-theory/#:~:text=Human% 20thoughts%2C%20feelings%2C%20and%20behaviours,and%20our%20relationships%20wit h%20it.

https://www.hsph.harvard.edu/nutritionsource/mindful-eating/#:~:text=Mindful%20eating%2 0focuses%20on%20your,your%20responses%20to%20those%20cues.%20%5B

https://mindowl.org/the-purpose-of-mindfulness/

https://www.edgewoodhealthnetwork.com/resources/blog/the-seven-pillars-of-mindfulness/

https://calmind.com/what-is-the-purpose-of-mindfulness/

https://bmcpsychiatry.biomedcentral.com/articles/10.1186/s12888-022-04356-6#:~:text=In% 20line%20with%20this%2C%20a,ended%20group%20treatment%20%5B50%5D.

www.ingramcontent.com/pod-product-compliance
Lightning Source LLC
Chambersburg PA
CBHW042316120626
46547CB00022B/2350